CW01018756

Understanding the Contact Centre Environment

David Mack & Claire Bateson

FINANCIAL
WORLD
Publishing

Financial World Publishing
4–9 Burgate Lane
Canterbury
Kent
CT1 2XJ

T   01227 818602
F   01227 479641
E   editorial@ifslearning.com

Financial World Publishing publications are published by The Chartered Institute of Bankers, a non-profit making registered educational charity.

The Chartered Institute of Bankers believes that the sources of information upon which the book is based are reliable and has made every effort to ensure the complete accuracy of the text. However, neither CIB, the author nor any contributor can accept any legal responsibility whatsoever for consequences that may arise from errors or omissions or any opinion or advice given.

Typeset by the Alden Group, Oxford.
Printed by Antony Rowe Ltd., Chippenham

ISBN 0-85297-637-2

Contents

Contents

Unit 1

Development of contact centres and their strategic use as a delivery channel

1.1
State the key issues affecting organisations which led to the call centre concept

The aim of Unit 1 is to enable you to:

1.1   *state the key issues affecting organisations which led to the contact centre concept;*

1.2   *explain the rationale for contact centres to meet customer needs and maintain shareholder value;*

1.3   *compare and contrast developments in technology which have allowed contact centres to grow in number and sophistication; and*

1.4   *explain the effects of emerging trends in the external environment and their likely impact on contact centre delivery*

This first section starts with a brief outline of the development of contact centres over the last 40 years.

The contact centre industry really got underway in the late 1980s and early 1990s. There are some in the home shopping sector who would argue that their call centre operations began long before the 1980s, as far back as the 1960s, albeit it that the services provided then were, in the main, relating to mail order. Many contact centres started life with just a few people using ordinary telephones arranged in a 'hunt' group (if the call is not answered by the first operator in a set number of rings the telephone system passes the call onto the next operator). This group of linked telephones could be contacted via one external telephone number. The employees did not think of themselves as contact centre advisers and often performed other clerical duties within a business. The team leader role often did not exist. This can be the way that contact centres start today in small organisations.

As the growth of other methods of communication have increased and the ease with which people can use them, the original 'call centre' which relied heavily on telephone communication, has given way to the term now used – 'contact centre'.

Think

How do you define a call centre?
How do you define a contact centre?

The classic definition of a call centre is a business or portion of a business that receives a large volume of incoming calls; these calls are answered automatically and passed to an adviser or placed in a queue until one becomes available. The types of calls are normally predictable and all advisers within the team have the ability to attend to caller requests. Simply put the term call centre is used to describe a way in which telephone calls are handled in a structured and consistent manner, through the use of set processes, practices and technologies.

A 'contact centre' takes this one step further and allows other electronic means of communication, such as e-mail.

In the beginning, the motive for setting up call centres was threefold, to:

- *reduce operating costs – there was a high cost involved in the 'bricks and mortar' element of the branch network for the financial services sector. There was also an inherent cost in staffing these branches which was a high proportion of organisation's operating costs;*
- *increase profit – by reducing costs, the profit (given that income did not decline) would increase. Also by providing a better, more accessible service to customers by using the telephone as a mean of communication, customers would be more likely to remain loyal and not to shop around to take their business elsewhere; and*
- *gain market share – one of the key indicators organisations are concerned with is the number of customers they can gain and retain. Improving your market share means that you will increase levels of income and be stronger against the competition.*

The ultimate aim was to encourage sales and make a better profit. Very little importance was put on customer care and meeting customers' expectations. Call centres had a more driven management approach and different goals.

Seizing hold of the prospect of cost reduction and increased profit, high street banks, building societies and insurance companies followed lead that First Direct had set in the late 1980s. First Direct was one of the first main financial service providers to offer banking through, as they were then, call centre operations. Through the closure of local branches the financial services industry grasped at the opportunity to reduce staff head-count and achieve significant cost savings through opening call centres. This also allowed the centralisation of much of their processing functions. Staff previously working within branches were offered employment within call centres or the new processing centres as an alternative to redundancy.

In the beginning, many call centre advisers were mainly young women. Although the roles tended to be repetitive, they required people skills rather than technical skills and so the profile of these new employees was different to that of the traditional 'banker'. This meant that little emphasis was placed on qualifications and so the absence of such did not preclude anyone from taking the roles. Shift patterns enabled advisers to fit in their job with home and family commitments.

These call centres were alleged to be the 'electronic sweatshops' of the 1990s. They were often likened to Victorian factories with workers subject to working in confined, restricted environments and working what was seen to be anti-social hours. To be a success, supervisors and call centre managers were tough on their workers, adopting dictatorial control. Employees were thought to suffer from high levels of stress, the level of job satisfaction was poor and the employees lacked motivation. The flat organisational structures meant that those wishing a career had little scope for progression.

Like most things, over time, contact centres have seen many changes, improvements and developments in working environments, policies and technologies. The majority of contact centres have moved away from the confined, congested working environment of the early years and now offer amiable, comfortable conditions. More men and more mature workers have joined the contact centre industry and the female : male ratio is changing. Although the work can still be repetitive and monotonous, job satisfaction is improving through multi-skilling programmes. With the increase in key industry sectors opening more contact centres this means there are more opportunities for the able contact centre adviser. This enables advisers to move form sector to sector and improve their job prospects and pay.

1.1.1 *Strategic direction and how it is formulated*

As we have said organisations set up contact centres to reduce operating costs; increase profit and market share, as well as offer an improved customer service.

Think

> What is a strategic decision?
> What are the issues that could be considered to be strategic?

A strategic decision is one which:

- *Affects the long-term direction of an organisation*
- *Tries to achieve an competitive advantage for the organisation*
- *Is concerned about the scope of the organisation's activities – should it stay in one sector or move into another one? What are the boundaries it sets itself?*
- *Matches the organisation's activities to the business environment in which it operates and the customers it serves. This is sometimes known as the 'strategic fit'.*

There will always be implications of strategic decisions. These may include the following.

- *Major resource changes in the organisation. This can be in terms of premises, staffing levels or choice of suppliers.*
- *Operational decisions, which could include management and control, geographic spread, distribution policies, marketing and advertising, personnel policies, etc.*
- *Values and expectations of stakeholders – stakeholders are the group of people who have an interest in the organisation and its activities. These most commonly include shareholders, management, the workforce, customers, suppliers and the local community.*
- *There will be an element of change in implementing new strategies and this too has to be managed for the new strategy to succeed.*

Question

What are the strategic issues that lead an organisation to consider setting up a contact centre?

The strategic issues could be as follows.

- High staff costs – *This can be linked to the geographical location of a business. Organisations are locating and relocating their business to regions worst hit by the loss of jobs in industries such as mining and manufacturing where labour is cheap and property and land are inexpensive. Contact centres will continue to be located in these regions in the UK for the very reason that the cost of running such an operation is more cost-effective. This has also led to businesses looking at overseas locations such as India.*
- The need to remain competitive – *one way of doing this is to cut costs by centralising of operations. This enables the reduction of property portfolios from numerous buildings around the UK or internationally to just one or two sites.*
- Changing customer lifestyles and expectations – *people now demand higher service in shorter timescales and are more willing to make use of the new technologies available to them. Customers are also more sophisticated and able to better understand the implications of purchasing different products and services.*

1.1.2 *Changing customer demands*

Traditionally customers shopped from a number of different shops located along the local high street. These shops specialised in their own products such as meat from the butcher, the baker for bread and cakes, fruit and vegetables from the green grocer, the cornershop for last-minute buys and so forth. The pace of life was slower and it was accepted that people had time to spend doing the shopping. Nowadays many customers lead busy lives and have little time for waiting and dealing with a large number of providers. There is more emphasis on leisure time and entertainment, which means that customers want convenience and accessibility.

Question

What type of service do consumers tend to seek to afford them maximum convenience?

Consumers prefer a 'one-stop-shop' where all their requirements can be met. This has seen in the rise of the popularity of supermarkets, where all goods can be obtained under one roof; and the decline of the cornershop and other similar shops who were unable to compete on price. With the improved purchasing power of these large organisations there is a greater variety and lower costs to the consumer. Shopping malls are also popular as consumers can find all their favourite shops within easy reach of each other. The ease of accessibility of these shops with good parking adds to their attraction.

Buying goods and services from the Internet has improved this accessibility and convenience as people can purchase goods and services from the comfort of their own home. The improvements in technology over recent years have improved payments over the Internet and allayed the concerns people have with this type of transaction.

When it comes to conducting personal finance transactions, customers no longer see the need to stand in a queue to withdraw, deposit or transfer money during their lunch hour. Customers are now demanding accessibility and flexibility from the bank they choose to do business with. They wish to access their account details, pay bills and transfer money at their convenience and to receive information in the format of their choice, using the communication media of their choice. Contact centres are evolving, and the growth is set to continue with the availability of more sophisticated technologies and increase in customer awareness.

As we move forward to a 24-hour society, and with the added ability of communicating via mixed media, such as e-mail, Internet based response forms and of course the traditional voice calls, the level of customer expectation is increasing. People demand service quicker and more efficiently. There is less of an expectation to pay for services, which has led to organisations looking at new ways to reduce costs.

Question

What are the benefits of the new ways of communicating and technology for customers?

These new and additional ways of communicating provide the customer with added benefits of convenience and choice. Customers realise that these advances in technologies offer them greater flexibility to browse and compare prices. They can shop at any hour of the day they choose. Customers are now accepting and embracing the new ways of communicating with their chosen supplier, whether it be for shopping, buying house or car insurance, paying bills or simply requesting information.

1.1.3 *Growth of new technology and the challenge faced by organisations wishing to use it*

The contact centre industry has, and will continue, to welcome with open arms advance in technology. Implementing new emerging technologies within a contact centre brings with it many challenges, not least the requirement for system reliability, which is by far the largest and most important factor. Organisations have to be prepared to face up to and deal with these challenges prior to bringing new technology into operation.

The majority of contact centres use an Automatic Call Distributor (ACD), a computerised system that routes incoming calls to the next available agent. Inevitably, developing and emerging technologies are becoming more sophisticated. Although still based upon the ACD, added benefits of integrated and automated systems and solutions have been introduced, providing voice processing and computer supported telephony applications.

As growth in development of technologies continues, contact centres are becoming more adventurous deploying Interactive Voice Response (IVR) and Computer Telephony Integration (CTI) systems and applications to front calls and route them to available agents with the right skill level or indeed handle calls fully without any human involvement at all. Developments will undoubtedly lead to more complex and sophisticated solutions. In the future, monotonous and simple telephone calls will be handled by technology, freeing up agents for the more sophisticated and complex calls. There will be a need to train and develop staff to deal in these new technologies and to deal with the more complex customer situations. There are also, for example, different skills sets needed to respond to customer e-mails than those required to deal with telephone conversations.

Question

What development in telephone technology has helped the increase of contact centres?

In the UK the much of the telephone network has been upgraded to a digital system. Relatively new technologies such as e-mail, the Internet, and Wireless Application Protocol (WAP) are now being utilised in contact centre operations. Developments continue with the 3G (3rd Generation), GPRS (General Packet Radio Service) and PDA (Personal Digital Assistant) technologies. Whilst the telephone remains the primary choice for customer communications, these additional ways of communicating are becoming more attractive as computers become cheaper to buy, processor and modem speed becomes faster and the cost of 'surfing' the Internet' lowers. The door has opened and made way for the Internet, the fastest and largest single delivery channel to enter the world of call centres in the last ten years.

Companies with existing contact centre operations need to carry out feasibility studies and budget planning when considering whether and how to implement new and additional technologies. There will be a considerable capital spend required to set up new sites, recruit and select the appropriate staff and the choice of the appropriate technology solution. Consideration will need to be given to existing processes and infrastructure to ensure that new services, solutions and technologies could be incorporated cost effectively. The return on the investment has to be justified.

1.1.4 New delivery channels, the decline of bricks and mortar and increased use of ATMs, AVR and telephone banking

The large high street presence of many organisations means that there will be a large amount of capital tied up in 'bricks and mortar'. The move by 'bricks and mortar' companies towards Internet-based and telephone-based customer contact centres will anticipate the reduction of costs. Such cost savings for these 'click and mortar' companies can be enormous.

The Internet has been the largest new delivery channel to emerge over the last ten years and it has even been suggested that the rise of the Internet will be the death of the contact centre industry. If the truth were known, the opposite is more likely to be the case. While the contact centre will have to evolve into a multimedia customer contact centre and agent roles will change, the industry has in fact found a new lease of life because of the Internet.

For the financial services industry, technology available now, together with that still emerging and developing, means they have good reason to turn away from the traditional trading methods of having a presence in every major town and city around the country. The industry, including banks, building societies and insurance companies, no longer sees the need for numerous expensive buildings, head offices and branches situated nationwide.

The cost of running a telephone or Internet service is lower than the traditional method of fully staffing high street branches throughout the country. The cost reduction is vast and organisations that have managed to successfully switch from the traditional methods are reaping the benefits. Today the financial services industry remains profitable whilst still being able to offer more products and services than ever before. More people are now handling their finances through new technologies rather than visiting their local branch.

Originally the introduction of the Automated Teller Machine (ATM) opened new doors for the general public with a new way of withdrawing money quickly and conveniently. An American company, Docutel, created the original ATM in 1969. The first ATM was installed in the wall of a New York bank. At that time ATMs could only dispense cash and worked offline. Banks were very cautious as to who had access to ATMs because there was no network connection between the bank and its ATM. The ATM had no way of checking the status of bank accounts. However, it was never the intention of its creators that the ATM would simply dispense cash and it was not what its customers wanted either. ATMs were created to do so much more than simply dispense money and in a very short space of time the technology evolved. In 1971 the 'total teller' was created and developed into the ATM we all know today.

With the developed technology, ATMs can now take deposits, transfer money between accounts, advance cash on credit cards as well as dispense cash and give account balances. ATMs can be found everywhere, not just on the outside wall of banks and are conveniently placed outside supermarkets, around shopping malls, retail parks, petrol stations, train stations and airports. ATMs work night and day, seven days a week, 365 days a year. In seconds, cash can be dispensed, bank balances checked, mini-statements provided, postal statements requested and money transferred. This means that the customer does not have to visit their branch in town, standing in a long queue at lunchtime. ATMs offer the customers of financial services organisations convenience, flexibility and all the services a high street branch can but without the hassle.

Following the ATM came telephone banking. The idea behind telephone banking was to offer a feasible, practical and workable solution and alternative to the traditional methods and ways of banking.

Question

Who was the first financial services provider to offer its services through a call centre?

A team was gathered together by Midland Bank (now HSBC) to look at the alternatives. From extensive external research the team was tasked to come up with ideas for a new way of banking that would put the customer first. They were tasked with eliminating the frustration customers felt with the traditional banking methods and, in addition, to find a solution that would offer the customer outstanding service and access.

In 1989 the result was unveiled to the general public, First Direct. It was the launch of an incredibly innovative way of banking and one that has set the scene and opened up a whole new world of banking for the general public. First Direct, the very first telephone bank, was virtually untried and untested when it launched. This new service enabled the customer to check account balances, hear details of recent transactions, and pay utility bills without the need to write out and post cheques. Moreover, these customers could automate bills by setting up regular payments, so that they could just sit back and relax rather than having to queue in the local branch. All of this could be done from the comfort of their home or work place. The service was an instant success and customers left the traditional providers in large numbers to subscribe to this new service.

With companies moving more towards telephone banking services, the need to retain investments in the form of buildings and the attendant head-count of staff has reduced. Telephone banking helped companies to centralise resources and customer service points were moved into contact centres. Financially, companies found it easier to maintain and run operations in this way than having to administer numerous small branches and offices around the country.

New developments offer more delivery channels for the contact centre industry;

effectively the new technology offers further communication media, more choice and more ways of doing business.

1.1.5 *Competition within the financial services industry, the threat from new players, consolidation through mergers and acquisitions and the growth of strategic alliances*

There are probably more technology applications for contact centres in a financial services institution than in any other kind of organisation. Because of the dynamic economic environment, financial services institutions must compete almost solely upon customer service. The fierce competition among the financial services providers' technology allows them to automate functions enabling operating costs to be keep to a minimum. By automating some or all of the more common functions the general operating overheads can be reduced enabling the financial service providers to pass these savings onto customers and improve shareholder value.

Question

What type of transactions can automated applications help financial service providers deliver?

Automated applications can help financial service providers with:

- *account opening and changing account details;*
- *account balance enquiries and statement browsing;*
- *interest rate enquiries;*
- *credit card authorisations;*
- *loan applications;*
- *out of hours service;*
- *stockbroking services;*
- *money transfers and bill payments; and*
- *general insurance.*

The traditional well-established financial institutions need to change the ways in which they now provide the common services to their current customer base. Customers now demand access to their accounts 24 hours a day and the ability to manage their account through the various channels already discussed. For financial services organisations this is a considerable change both in business process, culture and IT systems. For a new financial services provider starting from scratch some of these issues would not exist.

Question

What might the considerations an existing provider of financial services have to take into account when considering the implications of setting up a contact centre?

One issue for a financial services provider to consider in setting up a new contact centre might be the disposal of costly branch offices. A new financial services provider would start off with centralised staff, processes and systems eliminating the need to communicate with numerous branch offices and the most efficient and effective way of doing so. New players to the market would be more likely to introduce services to the customer faster and more efficiently as the systems they would have installed would cater for these new technologies; older organisations would need to change multiple legacy systems and/or databases – potentially a long and tortuous process. Whilst these older organisation make the necessary changes or integration they could find their customer base switching to the competition offering new, faster services which they would find hard to launch in the same timescales.

One way to increase an organisation's market share is through mergers or acquisitions where two organisations may decide to merge – effectively doubling the 'new' organisation's customer base overnight. Financially this would appear to be a quick and easy way of increasing customers. There does, however, need to be a lot of work in the background to ensure business processes are aligned, training is consistent throughout the new organisation, IT systems are fully integrated and communications are handled effectively. Another issue is the consolidation of staff or operational functions. In most case there is a reduction in staffing levels to eliminate duplication of work or functions and this has to be handled sensitively.

A common practice nowadays is to form strategic alliances with other companies who provide the same services, or companies which provides services which complement their current offerings. This enables a company to strengthen its position within its market without the need or expense of actually providing the new services internally from scratch. An example of this would be a new financial services provider, which already provides the standard savings and cheque accounts, that now wants to offer insurance or credit cards to compliment its existing services. Instead of setting up the new operation for credit cards it forms a strategic alliance with an existing credit card provider who provide the cards and manages the accounts on their behalf.

Summary

The key issues affecting organisations that led to the contact centre concept were born out of a desire to reduce costly overheads and to improve customer service. Strategically there was a need to met changing customer demands profitably and in a way that would deliver real competitive advantage. The growth of new technology has fuelled these demands and contact centres are very attuned to staying ahead of the game in this respect. The decline in 'bricks and mortar' has added to the restructuring of many high street organisations as new delivery channels spring up. Competition within the financial services sector will always ensure that this rate of change will increase rather that decrease.

1.2
Explain the rationale for contact centres to meet customer needs and maintain shareholder value

Contact centres meet customer needs by providing 24-hour service to the same high standard regardless of when the customer calls. Customers want availability, when it suits *them*. Traditional methods of delivering these services are not practical nowadays due to the accepted way in which people work in normal office environments.

The ability to deliver the best possible service using fewer resources, be it costly office space, people to process the requests or infrastructure to support the systems which process the requests, ensures that the company remains profitable. This in turn ensures the shareholders remain happy with a good return for their investment. Contact centres achieve this by maximising their profits by delivering a good grade of service using fewer costly resources. There is the need to deliver shareholder value, which in most cases means a good dividend and improved share price year-on-year.

1.2.1 *Enhanced service delivery through convenient, consistent processes and specialised staff*

Many transactions and processes can be standardised and therefore automated.

Question

How does automation benefit the customer?

This will ensure improved, efficient service, which is consistent, giving the customer a similar service experience regardless of who they are dealing with and where their call is routed to. This leads to a number of benefits to the organisation. The most costly part of establishing and running any business is staff. By automating as many processes as possible (training, call routing and even basic call answering) companies can save up to 70% on staff cost.

Question

How can technology help staff?

Technology can have a two-fold benefit for staff. Technology can help staff work productively and efficiently by taking away routine and boring tasks. It can also help to create a better working environment, for example, scheduling software that encourages advisers to take regular breaks. Staff are therefore more likely to be more enthusiastic and motivated, providing a better service to the customer. Happy and motivated staff are also more likely to remain loyal to the organisation.

Contact centres traditionally have a very high attrition rate, i.e. a very high turnover of staff. The costs involved in continuously recruiting and training new staff have serious implications for companies as it can cost up to twice the annual salary of the role the person is being recruited for. If the person does not stay in their role for this initial two-year period the organisation does not recoup the investment made in recruiting them. Investing in technology and software that is easy to use promotes a rewarding working environment therefore makes financial sense.

Staff training is still high on the list of important issues as their roles are highly specialised. Agents that benefit from effective training and scripted delivery will help to ensure that processes are consistently maintained. By investing in the tools to train staff such as combined computer and telephone interfaces, companies can reduce the need for one-to-one training and therefore manage training spend.

1.2.2 Investment in new delivery channels leading to cost base reduction; the effect of higher volumes of transactions and the effect on transaction cost per customer

The traditional call centre consisted of groups of agents taking many hundreds of telephone calls per day and providing a relatively good service. The key here is that the telephone was the main channel for voice calls. Since the 1990s there have been tremendous leaps and bounds in technology and the channels available.

Whilst the telephone remains the primary choice for customer communications, additional ways of communicating are becoming more attractive. Customers now have a choice of how they contact their financial service provider. These providers have the ability to offer customers a different ways of receiving information from them, SMS, WAP, e-mail, Internet, and of course, by telephone too.

The more ways the customer has to contact their financial service provider, the more efficient, more cost effective and more profitable the provider can become. How? Surely more contact with the bank will mean more people are required to service the customer? The majority of these new ways of communicating are automated; some take little or no effort at all on the customers' part, which in turn saves them money; and at the end of the day, the majority of people prefer financial service providers which will do just that. However, additionally, with all these new automated technologies financial service providers are now dealing with more and more customers each day. New technologies such as IVR, CTI and online banking allow providers to perform higher volumes of transactions each and every day. The majority of customers can perform transactions using these methods 24 hours a day, and they do. Financial service providers can also communicate with customers every hour of every day. They can automatically tell customers of their bank balance by SMS when the customer chooses, at the cost of around 10 to 12p a message it's very cost effective. Communicating and responding by e-mail reduces postage costs and gives a quicker, speedier response to customers. In addition, via the Internet financial services organisations can provide customers with the convenience of online banking at minimal operating cost.

By automating transactions financial services providers become more efficient, advisers do not need to get involved with day-to-day bill payments, customers can, and do, enjoy, controlling their accounts themselves. The benefits for the financial service providers are enormous. IVR and CTI applications, like the Internet, allow financial service providers the opportunity to handle higher volumes of transactions at minimal cost. The benefit to financial services organisations does not stop here. Higher volumes of transactions dealt with in real terms, means increased customer contact, which in turn leads to an increase opportunity to promote and sell new or additional products and services. However, higher volumes can mean increased stretch on resources and therefore increased costs if the service becomes very popular. The traffic therefore needs to be carefully monitored.

Question

What are the implications for the increased amount of automation on staff numbers and costs?

These new delivery channels can mean a reduction in staff, which in turn reduces overheads. Compare the cost of processing 10,000 balance enquiries, for example, using real advisers compared to processing the same number of requests using an IVR system. It will give exactly the same results, however it is far cheaper using technology rather than employing many hundreds of trained personnel.

1.2.3 *The importance of shareholder value and balancing the need to satisfy customers and shareholders*

Anyone who buys shares, even one share of stock in a company, can call themselves shareholders. One of the reasons companies 'float' on a stock exchange is to raise cash for their business. When a company first offers its common stock to the public this is called an Initial Public Offering (IPO). Once a company has floated its stock it then needs to ensure that it balances and satisfies the needs of both its customers and shareholders.

Shareholders are important and are valuable in that they help companies expand their market share. Shareholders provide companies with an injection of cash that increases working capital so that the company can expand its services. In return, shareholders can get invitations to the company's annual meeting and have the right to vote on the composition of the board of directors, as well as other company issues. They will benefit from a share of the profit in the form of dividends and hopefully improved value of the shares themselves. Shareholder value is important as organisations who are seen to consistently deliver this to shareholders will be easily able to raise cash on a stock exchange and to enjoy a good share value.

Customers will want good quality service and at the cheapest price. This means there will be a tension between the need to keep costs down to satisfy shareholders and to spend money on enhancing products and services to keep customers happy.

Question

How do contact centres contribute to providing shareholder value?

The ability to deliver the best possible service using fewer resources ensures that a company remains profitable, which ensures its shareholders remain happy with a good return for their investment. Contact centres achieve this by maximising their profits by delivering a good grade of service using fewer costly resources. This will be of benefit to the shareholders. This only half the picture, contact centres exist primarily to deliver excellent service to their customers, by providing good customer service, both the customer and shareholder needs are satisfied.

Summary

Contact centres are able to contribute to improved shareholder value by having the ability to automate customer requests, so leading to a more efficient and effective service. The new delivery channels enable organisations to find new ways to reduce costs and overheads. This reduction in costs leads to improved shareholder value, notwithstanding the need to provide a reliable and consistent service to customers.

1.3
Compare and contrast developments in technology which have allowed contact centres to grow in number and sophistication

Whilst the telephone remains the primary choice for customer communication, additional ways of communicating are becoming more attractive as computers become cheaper to buy and the cost of 'surfing' the Internet' lowers. The door has opened and made way for the Internet, the fastest and largest single delivery channel to enter the world of contact centres in the last ten years.

In the UK the telephone network has been upgraded to digital and relatively new technologies such as e-mail, the Internet, and Wireless Application Protocol (WAP) are now being utilised in contact centre operations. Developments continue with the 3G, GPRS and PDA technologies. The contact centre industry has and will continue to welcome with open arms advancement in technology.

1.3.1 Telephony systems, the different types, their advantages and disadvantages

Most modern contact centres will have a variety of systems depending on which market they are in. Within the financial services industry call centres will have at least an Automatic Call Distributor (ACD), which could be either a standalone ACD or a hybrid that will have ACD functionality as well as back office functionality.

Think

What type of system does your organisation use?

The main types of switching systems in a call centre are either standalone dedicated ACD platforms or a combination of ACD and PABX functionality, these are called 'hybrid switches'. Hybrid switching systems support different software applications on the same computer platform. Each provides the same basic functions but the hybrid offers a mixture of front and back office connectivity, where as the standalone dedicated ACD generally only offers front office functionality.

A standalone ACD would usually be linked into separate dedicated back office functionality, usually a PABX. A PABX is an automated system. Nowadays most of the connecting infrastructure, that is the links from the contact centre to the local exchange going into the public network, are digital. In the past connectivity would be via copper wires connected to the local exchange (known as 'analogue'). Digital connectivity is usually delivered via optical fibre; this method of delivery provides greater capacity of calls down to fibre connections. In comparison, 30 times the number of calls can be presented for the same physical space that a pair of copper wires takes up.

1.3.2 Centralisation of operations nationally to a few central locations and the pros and cons of doing so

A financial institution traditionally consisted of a central or head office building, with regional offices surrounded by hundreds of smaller branch or local geographical offices or locations. The costs in supporting these many hundreds of smaller locations would be very high. Prior to the emergence of contact centres companies had always considered the options of centralising their operations. However, due to the limitations of communications and the need for its customers to be served on a local basis this option has always proved to be problematic.

Originally call centres enabled the centralisation of core services due to the fact that the communication channel was the telephone. Customers did not have the need to visit a local office personally; they could talk to a company's staff using the telephone and get the same level of service as if they had visited the office. So why put in lots of small regional call centres when one national centre, or two call centres networked together could do the same job? In most industries that operate call centres the advantages of regional centres are overwhelming compared to the disadvantages.

Question

What are the advantages and disadvantages of a single centre?

Advantages of a single centre are as follows.

- *Better use of centrally located staff which reduces duplication of roles.*
- *Ease of training people located in one place, so reducing the costs of training.*
- *Less internal infrastructure to support the advisers contact centre software applications.*
- *Less hardware where back-up or duplication is required.*
- *More effective use of demographics, i.e. if there is one prime location in terms of population profile and salary costs.*

Disadvantages of a single centre are as follows.

- *A single point of failure be it the building, power, telecommunications or systems. Under a disaster situation the cost of recovering to a nearby suitable site can be extremely expensive. This is the biggest disadvantage.*
- *If the centre becomes overloaded then there is no spare capacity to take extra calls.*
- *There may be problems recruiting large quantities of suitable staff due to the location. Once all the available staff in the location have been employed then obviously the supply of suitable staff is exhausted.*
- *The success of one contact centre in the location may attract other organisations to the area and this will then lead to competition for resources.*
- *Staff will not have local customer knowledge.*

Summary

The main developments in technology stem from the use of digital telephone networks that can carry much large volumes of electronic data. There are various Automatic Call Distributor systems backed up with other software solutions that run back office processes. The question of fully centralising operations to one location can be seen, on the face of it, to be a reasonable idea, however, there are advantages to spreading operations and therefore spreading the risk should one site fail.

1.4
Explain the effects of emerging trends in the external business environment and their likely impact on contact centre delivery

The external business environment is undergoing constant change most of which is driven by the rate of innovation and acceptance of new technologies. This means that organisations have to invest in researching and developing new products and services and look at new ways reaching and serving customers.

Customers are becoming more educated and sophisticated and able to understand complex information about products and services. Added to this is the amount of regulation in place to protect consumers and the need for organisations to make product information available and transparent.

The following sections look at how technology is affecting contact centre delivery.

1.4.1 *E-Commerce – web enabling the delivery of service so that customers can access data themselves*

E-Commerce is an integrative concept, designed to draw together a wide range of business support services, including inter-organisational e-mail, directories, trading support systems for commodities, products, customised products and custom-built goods and services, ordering and logistic support systems, settlement support systems, and management information and statistical reporting systems.

Some people use the more restrictive terms 'electronic trading' and 'electronic markets', and others use broader terms such as 'electronic business'. Some people also restrict the scope of E-commerce to procurement; but it's more usefully conceived much more broadly, to include any kind of business-related transaction conducted with the assistance of electronic tools, even the telephone and fax.

E-commerce covers the following areas:

- *electronic business;*
- *electronic commerce;*
- *electronic publishing; and*
- *electronic services delivery.*

Electronic business

Electronic business is a useful general term for the conduct of business with the assistance of telecommunications and telecommunications-based tools. It comprises many overlapping segments, which are identified in the following sections.

Electronic commerce

Electronic commerce (e-Commerce) is commonly described as a way of trading and paying for goods and services on the Internet. It has developed with the assistance of telecommunications and telecommunications-based tools. Additionally, with the introduction of web applications, it is e-Commerce that has allowed and enabled customers to access their own data and service their own accounts across the Internet. This in turn has helped financial service providers to reduce unnecessary head-count in their contact centres.

Some people use the term 'electronic trading' to mean much the same thing as e-Commerce. Others use 'electronic procurement', 'electronic purchasing' or 'electronic marketing'. Note, however, that e-Commerce is often used in a much broader sense, to mean essentially the same as 'electronic business', as defined above. Examples of electronic business that are *not* e-Commerce include registration and licensing processes, student enrolment, and court administration.

Note that e-Commerce comprises many segments, some of which have their own names. For example:

- *'electronic catalogues' refers to means whereby sellers can communicate their offerings to potential buyers;*
- *'electronic data interchange' (EDI) refers to a particular family of standards for expressing the structured data that represent e-commerce transactions; and*
- *'electronic auctions' for a particular set of mechanisms for setting prices.*

Electronic publishing

Electronic publishing is usefully defined as electronic commerce in digital goods and services that are intended for consumption by the human senses, not just the written word. It encompasses a range of formats, including text, structured data, image, both raster/bit-map and vector, moving image (animation and video), sound, and combinations of the above ('multimedia').

Electronic services delivery

Electronic services delivery (ESD) is usefully defined as e-commerce in services, i.e. the provision of services with the assistance of telecommunications and telecommunications-based tools. ESD excludes traffic in physical goods, and hence is concerned with applications of electronic business where, at least in principle, the entire activity can be performed electronically.

Question

What type of services could be classed as ESD?

The term is commonly used to refer to government applications of e-Commerce. It is also used in relation to such industry sectors as banking and other financial services, trading in commodities, reservations for travel and entertainment events and distance learning.

All the services described are available via channels that can be easily accessed by customers, usually the world wide web, and can then access their own data without the need to interact with another person.

1.4.2 Multi-channel delivery – provision of choice

Today's financial services industry is evolving more quickly and dynamically than ever. The drive to improve customer acquisition and retention while containing costs means that, financial institutions need flexible, scalable and reliable systems that deliver the right products and services, at the right time, through any channel. Banking and securities are blending together, resulting in a broader range of services and a wider target customer base. Financial services companies are fortifying their core strengths while entering new markets. They live with intense pressure from both traditional and non-traditional competitors that threaten their profitable lines of business and force substantial marketplace changes. In this race, technology plays a critical role in the drive to differentiate and compete. While reinforcing their trusted and established role for both commercial and retail clients, financial institutions are deploying next generation solutions that meet the rapidly changing needs of these clients.

Question

What are the main concerns of consumers when they are using these new technologies?

Customers expect secure access to financial information anytime, anywhere from any device. And the most important element to all this is that the systems installed to deal with all this customer activity is stable and reliable. Resilience is key to network stability and system reliability. Without this the consumer will not trust the new technologies and what they can deliver. With the availability of secure and reliable technology, financial service providers can now meet the technology expectations of their customers via a multi-channel delivery system that leverages the power of the Internet, wireless technology, and service-driven networks.

1.4.3 SMS text messaging, WAP phones and Digital TV

While the majority of customer contact centres by telephone or e-mail, new communication methods are fast evolving. This next section outlines a few of the newest developments.

The Small Message Service (SMS) has been introduced in many contact centres as a useful and cost effective method of delivering information to and communicating with customers. SMS is more commonly known as text messaging or text messages and is available for users of mobile phones using Global System for Mobile (GSM) networks. The service allows mobile phone users to send and receive text messages of up to 160 characters. These are sent and received via the network operator's message centre to your mobile phone, or from the Internet, using a so-called 'SMS gateway' website. If the phone is powered off or out of range, messages are stored in the network and are delivered at the next opportunity. Organisations can now send information to customers regularly advising them of new services or products, special deals and offers and send headline news. In the financial services industry customers can now opt to receive regular mini-statements, bank balances and recent transaction information via SMS. They can also choose to be forewarned that they are nearing a nil balance, credit limit or overdraft limit. Some organisations offer to send a message via this service informing customers of share prices on a regular basis. For the majority of organisations, SMS technology is a very economical communication channel with very little outlay. For the customer, there is generally no charge for the service and once set up, very little input from them is required. As the service is usually automated, very little input is required from the organisation either.

Wireless Application Protocol (WAP) technology was the creation of four companies, Motorola, Nokia, Ericsson and Unwired Plant. It is a worldwide standard in mobile phone software that allows you to read specially written Internet pages directly on the screen of your digital phone. This means that WAP allows users to access the Internet, interact with information and services and send e-mail instantly via wireless devices such as mobile phones and two-way radio transceivers. WAP utilises the Wireless Markup Language (WML) to create pages that can be delivered to these devices. WAP enabled devices that can display and access the Internet to use a special type of browser called 'micro browsers', which has small file sizes that can accommodate the low memory and low bandwidth constraints of handheld devices and wireless handheld networks.

With WAP, new developments and features are being built all the time. WAP literally puts the Internet in your pocket, so the potential benefits are as wide as the Internet itself. A WAP phone is all you need to search out information such as news, weather, sports results, stock prices and exchange rates, flight timetables and hotel information. Soon, you'll also be able to carry out transactions and purchases from your phone. This means being able to buy travel or theatre tickets, book hire cars, make reservations, pay bills and trade shares, wherever you are, using only your phone. By logging onto the Internet using wireless handheld devices, such as their mobile phone, customers can access their account details at any time, retrieving bank balances, and recent transaction information. Additionally, customers can pay bills and transfer money between accounts by simply using the keypad. For the financial services industry, WAP technology presents an additional delivery channel offering convenience and security to the customer. Once implemented requires limited resource to operate. The financial services industry now offers the ability for customers to use such devices to take care of banking arrangements.

Question

What are the downsides of using a WAP phone to view the Internet?

There are downsides of using a WAP phone to view the Internet even though much of the information of the Internet can be viewed on a mobile phone using WAP. This is because the rich graphical experience we have become familiar with on the world wide web can't be displayed on a small handset screen. The other main difference is navigating between pages – there's no mouse to point and click so you need to scroll between options using up/down keys, and 'click' by pressing an 'OK' button.

Interactive Digital Television (iDTV) was first launched in the winter of 1999 by a combination of service providers including Sky, BT, HSBC and Japanese company Matsushita. IDTV allows viewers to interact with their television set via a telephone line (land line) or network TV cable connection. At launch interaction was fairly limited and in the main used for shopping and basic banking services. Today, it offers users the opportunity to browse, shop, bank, book holidays, send and receive e-mails and much more.

IDTV has opened up another route for communications between the financial services industry and their customers. Now customers can check their bank balances, mortgage and saving accounts, credit card statements, ISAs, TESSAs and unit trusts in between watching their favourite television programmes. 'Armchair' banking now enables customers without access to a personal computer or an Internet connection, without a WAP enabled mobile phone or handheld wireless devices, to carry out day-to-day banking administration, pay bills and transfer funds with the minimum of inconvenience and in the comfort of their own homes.

The future will see additional ways of communication between organisations and customers, as emerging technologies come to fruition. Waiting in the wings are technologies such as 3G and GPRS. Further, but in the not too distant in the future are technologies such as Extended Messaging Service (EMS) and Multimedia Messaging Service (MMS). EMS will allow text messages to be extended beyond the current 160-character limit and for users to send and receive simple sounds and animated graphics. MMS technologies will go a few steps further. With an MMS enabled mobile users will have the ability to send and receive messages with text and graphics, audio and video clips as well as photographs.

Currently, and for the foreseeable future, however, there is no replacement for the telephone. Research has shown that despite new technologies contact via the telephone still remains the number one delivery channel into call centres.

Summary

Emerging trends in the external environment show that the technological rate of change is ever increasing. This seems to be having a positive impact on contact centre delivery as providers innovate to accommodate the new delivery channels. E-Commerce is allowing customers to increase their ability to 'self-serve' with their choices of how to do this being very wide. Underlying all these technological innovations is the need to ensure that the supporting systems are reliable and resilient. Without this the consumer will not trust the new technologies that are emerging.

Unit 2

Information Technology and Managing Information within the Contact Centre

2.1
State the differences in contact centre technology infrastructure and the relationships between telephony and contact centre software

Contact centre technology has changed dramatically over the past 15 years. Early call switching systems were physically very large, consumed enormous amounts of power, produced enough heat to keep the contact centre warm, were noisy in their operation and difficult to configure and maintain. With the advances in microchip technology and the availability of these products the systems required to run a small contact centre could be the equivalent size of a small suitcase.

Within a contact centre there are various types of technology used to provide the ability to effectively route incoming calls to advisers. In the past contact centre technology was based on an analogue platform which is now virtually redundant. Today all contact centre platforms are based on digital speech technology.

In modern contact centres, speech is switched in time as opposed to physical relays or connectors switching incoming calls to advisers. Since the advent of digital connections from the local exchange, the majority of contact centres are now fully digital from the exchange through to the switching platform to the point where advisers answer the call.

Platforms, on which the contact centre software is hosted, differ between manufacturers. The two main platforms are either UNIX based processor or NT based server. Automatic Call Distributor (ACD) manufacturers are moving over to NT based platforms to provide an open interface to third-party suppliers.

2.1.1 *Main types of system*

Most modern contact centres will have a variety of systems depending on which market they are in. Within the financial services industry contact centres will have at least an ACD, which could be either a standalone ACD or a hybrid that will have ACD functionality as well as back office functionality.

The main types of switching systems in a contact centre are either standalone dedicated ACD platforms or a combination of ACD and PABX (private automatic branch exchange system) functionality, these are called 'hybrid switches'. Hybrid switching systems support different applications on the same platform. Each switch provides the same basic function but the hybrid offers a mixture of front and back office connectivity, whereas the standalone dedicated ACD generally only offers front office functionality.

A standalone ACD would usually be linked into separate dedicated back office functionality, usually a PABX. Most of the connecting infrastructure, that is the links from the contact centre to the local exchange going into the public network nowadays are digital (see section 1.3).

For a primarily outbound contact centre an essential piece of equipment would be a 'powerdialler'. Powerdiallers come in various forms and enable contact centres to make a large volume of outbound calls. There are a number of methods in which they work:

- manual dialling – *using the keyboard or keypad to place calls;*
- screen dialling – *dialling from an object on the screen (e.g. name, number) and receiving an indication of the call progress on the screen;*
- pre-view dialling – *a list of customers to be called is maintained by the computer system and the call list or data pertaining to the next person to be called is presented to the adviser. The adviser then initiates the call by a simple indication (e.g. by clicking a 'go' button) or by using screen or manual dialling;*
- power dialling – *the power dialling controller has a list of numbers to be called, a number of outgoing telephone lines and a group of advisers. It launches as many telephone calls as it possibly can and, as soon as an answer is detected on a particular line, attempts to connect the call to an adviser. If no adviser is free it drops the answered call and launches another. Note that the powerdialler and its more civilised relative, the predictive dialler, detects and removes all calls that are not*

answered or completed for any reason. It will also detect fax machines and attempt to detect answering machines, ensuring, where possible, that advisers do not waste their time on these devices;

- *progressive dialling – here at least one adviser must be free before a call is launched. The controller detects that an adviser is free, selects the next call to be made and makes it. The call will either be connected directly to the free adviser or will be connected when answer is detected, as in power dialling; and*

- Predictive dialling – *predictive dialling is similar to power dialling but is far more subtle. It is a compromise between power and progressive dialling in its effect. Here, rather than launching a mass of telephone calls regardless of the adviser availability as the powerdialler does, the controller uses a 'pacing algorithm' such that the rate of launch is based upon the probability of an adviser being free. The predictive dialler tries to predict the precise time to launch a call such that an adviser will be free within a specified period of the call being answered (say one second).*

2.1.2 *Factors in design*

Many factors come into play when designing a contact centre and the technology within it. There are five primary factors; the cost of the equipment, how resilient the solution should be, the amount of traffic (volume) the contact centre will need to handle, whether the site will be a single standalone or networked with other call centres and how or what support functionality will be required.

Breaking these down further, taking each in order, cost will always be an important factor. Although it shouldn't be the most important factor, in reality it will be. The budget for establishing a contact centre, and particularly its technology, will determine the functionality of the ACD platform. This will also affect what associated peripherals the ACD will have, such as statistical reporting, voice recording, wall boards, visual indicators, connectivity into remote databases, the ability to introduce CTI and IVR functionality. All these peripherals greatly increase the cost of a basic system. Equally, systems that support all of this functionality and that have connectivity are generally far more expensive than a basic ACD platform.

Resilience is an important factor depending on how 'mission critical' a contact centre will be. If the contact centre needs to run for 24 hours, seven days a week with virtually no down time, then providing a resilient solution will be paramount to that company. Resilience can be designed into contact centres either by multiple platforms, dual processors running within a single platform, the way in which the infrastructure is delivered into a building and standby power in case of loss of mains into a building, to name but a few.

The traffic, or volume of calls, delivered to the contact centre is another major factor. A contact centre handling a small volume of calls will only require a small number of advisers, consequently an entry level ACD will be adequate to handle the incoming calls. As the volume of calls increase to thousands of calls a day, the ability to process and deliver these calls to the advisers increases. The need to service these calls more frequently with comfort messages and potentially music on hold requires powerful switching platforms, increasing the cost of the platform and the sophistication of software on it.

If a contact centre needs to be linked to other centres, either to distribute the calls or to provide a seamless experience for the incoming caller regardless of where a centre is located geographically, then this factor will determine the type and manufacturer of the platform to be used. Different platforms provide different types of connectivity between them and these protocols determine the functionality between contact centres.

As a contact centre grows and or a contact centre network expands the support of these systems and the infrastructure connecting them needs to be taken into consideration, as this will be an important factor particularly for a 24 hours a day, seven days a week operation. A contact centre that operates during working hours will have the benefit of carrying out maintenance work during the night, whereas a typical 24 : 7 operation has a very limited window of opportunity to rectify any problems or make changes to call routing or network routing. These are important factors when designing a contact centre.

2.1.3 *How the technology works*

The majority of contact centre platforms use a sophisticated software program to handle incoming calls and deliver them to the advisers within the call centre. Incoming calls are delivered on channels or 'trunks' and are usually answered automatically by the ACD platform if no advisers are available. Comfort messages are provided informing the customer of any potential delays or offering general information. The contact centre platform will deliver the call once an agent becomes available. Most contact centre software applications will deliver the longest waiting call to the longest waiting adviser.

The sophistication of this software has developed over many years. Initially the queuing 'algorithms', the term used for queuing calls, were based on simple call switching principles but as time progressed and the increase in contact centres was apparent, ACD manufacturers developed more complex algorithms with far greater user definable parameters. Long gone are the days when only the manufacturer can change the way in which the system operates. It is now normal for administration staff within the contact centre to completely reconfigure these systems without the need for an engineer to assist. Manufacturers have made the user interface to the ACD more 'user friendly' making the configuration tools similar to the style and functionality as the administrator would use during their normal working day. Simple 'drop and drag' tools using graphics and icons to represent, what in the past, would have been line after line of complex code.

With the introduction of Computer Integrated Telephony (CTI) and Interactive Voice Response (IVR) manufacturers are moving to an open architecture. CTI, in its simplest form, is the technology which replaces some or all of the processing of calls away from the core ACD software, to an external computer which has the ability to run complex bespoke routing and/or voice applications

Perhaps the simplest thing to do is to disconnect the telephone from the line and plug in a computer. This is the beginning of first-party CTI. What happens when you plug the computer into the line? First of all you need the right plug, which means that the computer must have a telephone line 'interface' or contact point. Given that interface and some suitable software, the computer can do everything that you could do with your telephone. It can make calls, take calls and manipulate calls. Normally it will do that under your control – but your interface can be much better than this. Screen-based telephony will allow you to make calls directly from your database and call-based data selection can be used to 'pop' useful information onto your screen, based on the caller's identity before you answer an incoming call. This gives a couple of examples from the seven generic functions of CTI.

Naturally, having made or received a call, in the normal course of events, you wish to speak to the person at the other end of the line. This requires a telephone. One option is to use the old telephone by plugging it into the computer. This means that the computer has to have a telephone socket or interface. Where the telephone is separated from the computer in this way the approach to CTI is called 'discrete first-party', because the building blocks are unchanged, they are simply connected differently. An alternative is to turn the computer into a telephone, perhaps by using a soundboard with its microphone and loudspeakers. This is 'merged first-party'. The building blocks have physically integrated. Figure 1.1 illustrates the difference between discrete and merged first-party CTI.

Note that in first-party CTI the computer is connected to the telephone line just as the normal telephone is. Hence the first-party CTI computer only sees whatever the telephone sees and can only do what the telephone does. The telephone system is not aware of this form of CTI. However, the telephone system does offer different interfaces according to the telephone that it thinks is connected. The overall process is depicted in Figure 1.1.

The basic POTS telephone has a simple signalling protocol. The line is looped when a person wishes to make a call, digits are sent to specify the telephone number, a ring tone is returned and so on. This is basic signalling. There are other telephones, feature phones and key phones, for example, that have enhanced

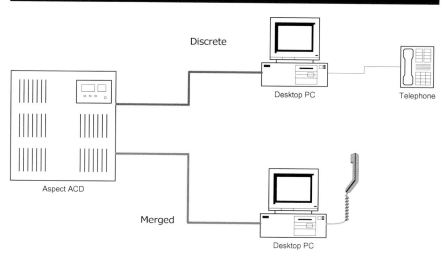

Figure 1.1

signalling. A feature phone may let people conference a call with a single button. A key phone will let a person see what other people in the group are doing. These are important enhancements so far as the first-party CTI computer is concerned. It can then provide much more information on the progress of calls and offer many more functions. Thus first-party CTI can be of two types, 'enhanced' or 'basic', according to which type of telephone line that the computer is connected to. The overall picture for first-party CTI then becomes:

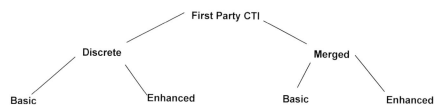

The implementation for merged first-party is generally via a plug-in PC card; the card can use any of the 'bus' (messaging) structures that are in place: ISA, PCMCIA, PCI, etc. The card usually deals with a single line only, though it can connect to more. This same option can be used for discrete, but there are alternatives. The hardware that sits between the line and the telephone is, in this instance, called a 'line intercept'. Though the technology is much the same in all cases the line intercept can be placed in the telephone, in the PC or in a separate box. Figure 1.2 illustrates these arrangements.

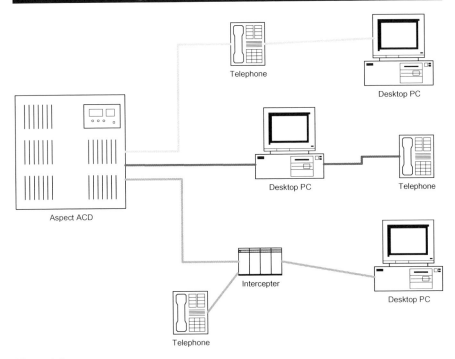

Figure 1.2

The approach chosen is sometimes predetermined. If all of a computer's card slots are full then a separate box may make sense. If there are no external ports (sockets) free on the computer then the card may be the only practical solution. If the telephone already has a data capability then a phone-based solution will be cheapest, and so on. If the choice is not predetermined then the computer card solution is often preferred. This is because it can provide a merged solution and because it often offers more than basic CTI functionality; many of the cards have voice processing capability.

Third-party control

First-party CTI is so called because the computer is replacing you, or acting for you, and you are the first-party in the call. People often ask who the second party is. The second party, though we do not generally refer to it as such, is the other party in your call. The calling or called party is the second part. Who then is the third-party? In human terms the third-party in a call is normally the telephone operator, receptionist or attendant. The operator takes, makes or manipulates the call on behalf of the first and second parties. The operator takes no part in the call itself. When a call arrives, the operator answers it, asks the caller who they wish to be connected to, connects the call and then leaves it to the two parties. Usually the operator deals with many calls during your particular call. The operator is a central resource, usually having the capability to observe and control all the lines on the 'switch'.

The third-party computer is just like the operator in most respects. It is a central resource with the ability to observe and control all of the lines of the switch. It does not take part in the calls. It simply makes them, takes them and manipulates them. It may do this because an application belonging to an individual user requests it to do so, or because some central application does so.

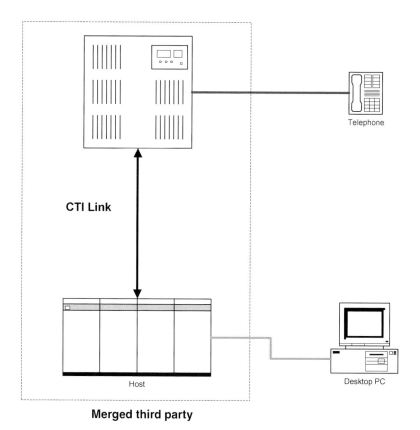

Merged third party

Figure 1.3

Precisely as the operator requires a special interface to the switch, so too does the third-party computer. This is the third-party CTI link. The link itself and the protocol (rules of operation) that exists on it belong to the switch supplier. Most CTI links are proprietary just as operator console interfaces are generally proprietary. Note that the link carries messages between the computer and switch – it is not there to carry calls. The general arrangement for a third-party CTI system joins the building blocks as shown in Figure 1.3.

The physical connection does not take place at the desktop here. The association between any individual telephone and terminal is a logical one, whereas it is a physical one in first-party. This means that the addresses of the telephone and terminal that are linked for CTI purposes are held in a table within the computer. Hence the concept of merging at the desktop is not particularly meaningful in third-party CTI. Centralised merging does make sense though. This merges the switch and computer into one, as shown in the dotted lines in Figure 1.3.

This arrangement applies to the computer mainframe where the terminals are 'dumb' (they are an input device only) and all intelligence is concentrated into the computer of Figure 1.3. So what of the more common arrangement – client server? Diagrammatically the arrangement for client server CTI is little different. As shown in Figure 1.4, the computer has become a CTI Server and the terminals are connected via the LAN (local area network) and have become PCs.

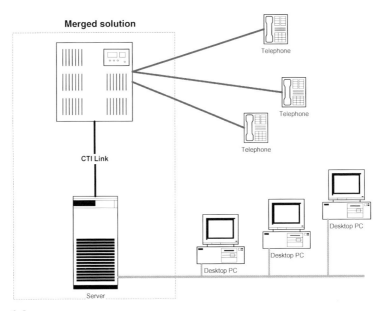

Merged solution

Telephone

Telephone

Telephone

CTI Link

Desktop PC

Desktop PC

Desktop PC

Server

Figure 1.4

However, though Figure 1.4 shows that there are no major topological differences, this does tend to disguise this software arrangement. Now that the terminals are PCs then part or all of the CTI application may be located there rather then in the centralised server. Note that Figure 1.4 still shows the merged option. Here the CTI Server and switch have combined.

Third-party CTI does not interface to a telephone line so there are no signalling system variants here. There are however some types of third-party which are mostly concerned with the nature of the nature of the CTI link and the messages that flow across it. At the present time the most common type is 'third-party compeer'. Here the computer (or server) and switch communicate as equals across a CTI link that is specially designed for that communication. The switch and computer are aware of the CTI implementation.

It is possible to connect a third-party computer to a switch that is not CTI-aware. Switches bristle with interfaces that provide information to management systems and take commands from them. These can be used to create primary third-party CTI systems. In other primary arrangements the computer pretends to be a PBX, trapping the calls then passing them on to the PBX itself. This too is a third-party primary solution – but it does require that the computer actually carries calls. Third-party primary solutions are useful where the switch has no CTI link or where the upgrade costs of providing a link are excessive.

The third type of third-party CTI is called 'dependent'. In third-party dependent CTI the switch is dumb. It relies on the computer for instructions on how to deal with all calls that it switches. The software that allows a normal switch to control calls is referred to as 'call processing'. In third-party dependent CTI call processing has been moved from the switch to the CTI computer. Third-party dependent CTI is particularly relevant in merged systems but also exists in discrete form. The Summa Four SDS-1000 is an example of a dumb switch, it has a special protocol called 'Host Control Link' which provides full control to an external computer. In merged systems the switch is usually implemented on cards within the PC. There is no link as such and the cards are clearly unable to process calls themselves.

The linking options for third-party CTI is summarised as follows. The options apply to both mainframe and client server implementations.

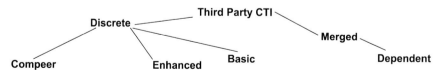

The choice of third-party approach depends on many factors. Primary solutions are usually dictated by the lack of a CTI link or cost considerations. Dependent implementations are claimed to provide flexibility by focusing control at one point. Merged systems are still rare; the argument for them may be economic but they do not currently offer significant cost savings. Most implementations use compeer at present; implementers are often protected from the vagaries of a world which is mostly proprietary by the application programming interface.

Voice processing systems

All of the voice processing systems that are commonly used are really much the same. Where the systems differ is in the applications, the interfaces supported and in the size of the system.

Here is a simple categorisation based on interfacing:

Voice processing systems

Voice response units   Interactive voice response   Voice messaging systems
                                          units

All voice processing systems interface to the telephone system. They might interface to analogue or digital lines and might use any of a large number of signalling systems, but they all have these interfaces in common. Where the categories of voice processing systems really do differ are shown in the following table:

Table 1.5

Voice processing system	Extra interfaces	Example applications
Voice response units	None	Voice announcements Call sequencing Audiotex Interactive audiotext Voice forms Voice routing
Interactive voice response	Computer system	Transaction processing e.g. Automatic banking Order processing Web page access
Voice messaging systems	Switch integration LAN	Telephone answering Automated attendant Integrated messaging Voice mail

Clearly the voice response unit is the most basic of the three. It has the most basic interface in that it simply connects to the telephone system, but there are still plenty of things that it can do.

Voice response units

Most people have been in contact with a number of voice response units. For example, the simple railway timetable announcement, the weather report and the routing function supplied by numerous service industries which allowed you to access a help desk, etc. All of these are based on voice processing units. The routing function is worth dwelling on for a moment.

There are many different ways in which this could have been achieved without the use of a voice processing system. A company could, for example have allocated a specific number for each of the functions. The switch could then be used to route the calls using direct dialling-in (DDI, DID) digits. Using the voice response unit a company does not have to publish lots of different numbers and can add new services or take old ones away, simply by reprogramming the unit. As this implementation has no special interfaces then the only way that it can route calls is by transferring them. Just as a telephone user would. This is rather like first-party CTI.

It can be inefficient where the specific switch does not support 'blind' transfer. Here the voice response unit has to stay with the call until it is answered. Some voice response units have built-in switches that get around this problem, but this is not always efficient. However, if the switch itself has a CTI line then the computer could re-route the calls. This would require an interface between the voice response unit and the computer, which transforms it into an interactive voice response system. Some voice response systems interface directly to the CTI link themselves; in this case they become CTI 'servers'.

Interactive voice response

Interactive voice response systems are important in a CTI context. This is an area where small CTI can work well with voice processing to produce systems that are both automated and integrated. However, many Interactive Voice Response (IVR) systems have no integration. Where an IVR system is working to a mainframe or legacy system then the most common interface is via 'terminal emulation'. The computer is not aware that the IVR system is anything more than a terminal. This simple set up is shown below.

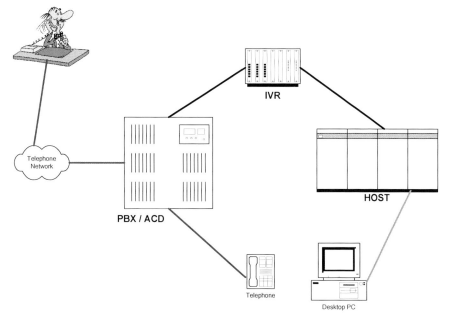

Figure 1.6

In a modern system the IVR may connect to a database through a LAN. In this case it may use one of the many means of accessing that database that exist in client server computer world, anything from SQL to ODBC. The point once again is that the database server is not aware that the IVR system is anything special; it is just another client.

Voice messaging systems

Table 1.5 lists switch integration and the LAN as the distinguishing interfaces here. The latter is only used in integrated messaging which will be covered later. Both are shown in Figure 1.7.

The basic connection to the switch is exactly the same as that used in connecting a telephone extension. The special part of this arrangement is the integration interface. Its purpose can be grouped under the general title 'message exchange'. This interface is not a CTI link. Its functions are given in Table 1.5.

Not all the functions listed are supported on all switches, the use of call type and caller identification being more sophisticated options. Note that the telephone answering functionality offered by a voice messaging system is worse then that provided by an answering machine if the system is not integrated.

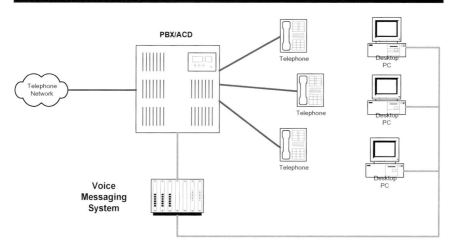

Figure 1.7

Switch integration is implemented in many different ways. The only standard here is the Simple Message Data Interface from Bellcore, which is used in some Centrex implementations. Most switches have their own way of delivering the functions listed in Table 1.8. Here are some examples:

- *data link;*
- *feature phone signalling;*
- *tone before ringing;*
- *tone after ringing; and*
- *inter-PBX link.*

It should be clear that telephone answering and voice mail are complementary applications. Voice messages are left as a result of telephone answering or deliberately sent as a message. The basic functions of the voice mail application are the so-called RSPFR functions. The letters stand for the functions required to:

- **r**ecord messages;
- **s**end them to one or a number of other mail-boxes;
- **p**lay messages;
- **f**orward them to someone else or; and
- **r**eply directly to the sender.

Systems do have a great many other features but it is the RSPFR set which really gets used. The basic voice mail functions can be likened to the basic functions needed to make and receive calls in normal telephony. There exists, of course, a multitude of supplementary features in voice mail, just as there is in telephony.

Table 1.8

Application	General function	Notes
Telephone answering	Mailbox identification	The interface usually delivers the number that the caller dialled. The system can then translate this into a specific mailbox number so that the system can route the call directly to the correct mailbox and then use the owner's greeting.
	Call type	The call type can be used to provide different responses depending upon whether the called party is on a call or not replying, for example.
	Call identification	The caller identification can be used to vary the response given or to tag a received message with the calling number.
Auto-attendant	Call waiting return	If a call that is delivered by an attendant is not answered within a specific time the call is usually returned to the attendant. This may be an internal function, in which case the call will not be returned via the integration interface.
Voice mail	Message delivery	The user has to be informed that there are messages in the mailbox in most applications – whether those calls originate from the telephone answering or direct messaging using voice mail. The switch may respond to a message waiting indication by various means including lighting a lamp on the telephone or activating a pager. Message delivery also covers reception of the message. In some cases the system may forcibly deliver the message. More often the user calls into the system to listen to the messages that are in the mailbox.

Integrated messaging

The simplest way to indicate that a voice message has arrived is to cause a lamp to light beside the telephone. However, if the voice messaging system is connected to a LAN, as it is in Figure 1.7, then all of the functions listed in Table 1.8 can be sent via the LAN. For example, individual message waiting indications can be sent to individual PCs. This option begins the move into the world of integrated messaging. E-mail on the PC is usually viewed as an in-tray. The messages are text-based and the in-tray displays useful information about them, such as: arrival time, name of sender, length, etc. An integrated message in-tray simply extends the scope to cover voice and fax messages. The in-tray contents can be built up from voice and fax message waiting indications sent across the LAN from the voice processing system.

Text messages are accessed simply by pointing and clicking the mouse; this causes the relevant file to be opened and its contents to be displayed to the screen. What happens when a voice message is opened? This message must be delivered to the telephone, so a command must pass across the LAN to the voice messaging system that causes the voice message to be delivered to the correct telephone. Alternatively, the message sent across the LAN can be played at the computer. Many issues can arise, for example, how will the message be played? Furthermore what happens when you are away from the office? Can the message be recovered via a normal telephone? It also opens up other opportunities: delivering e-mail via a text-to-speech synthesiser, or a spoken indication that a fax has arrived. In the latter case the user may be able to hear who the fax is from and then redirect it to a nearby fax machine.

Integrated messaging products are currently targeted at individual users but there are clearly applications in the contact centre environment. Nowadays applications are capable of alerting or delivering messages via many varied channels. A simple e-mail, as described above, would have normally sufficed but with the increase use of Short Message Services (SMS) and the wide spread use of mobile devices more and more customers want to have the ability to use any or all of the available methods. Messages can be delivered via e-mail, SMS, fax, automated voice applications or a normal contact centre adviser.

2.1.4 *Advantages and disadvantages of each*

The variety of systems currently available offers a huge range of features and facilities which all have their advantages and disadvantages.

The advantages of the systems currently available are as follows.

- Open architecture – *this is proving to be extremely useful for corporations that intend to develop their own sophisticated call routing and/or voice application. An open architecture means that the main ACD system can integrate into various external computer systems or databases without the need to develop bespoke software to integrate them together.*

The idea of computer and telephony convergence is nothing new. Companies have used computer telephony integration (CTI) links to connect their computing and phone systems together for well over a decade – and many have gained significant benefits in terms of improved productivity and reduced costs. PC-based voice and fax processing systems have also been developed for years.

From both a business and a technology point of view, computer technology makes perfect sense. Why have IT and telephone systems in an organisation that don't talk to each other? Especially when through integration – or through migration of communication and computing systems over to a common computing platform such as WinNT – a company can enable new applications and gain significant benefits.

What has mainly held back the adoption of CT has been its slow take-up among the computer developer community. Finding a team of computer programmers to write a suite of business applications for your enterprise is relatively straightforward. But finding a team of developers with sufficient knowledge of both the telephony and computing words to build a suite of CT applications that integrate voice, fax, video, Internet and speech technologies is a different proposition.

There are two obvious solutions to this dilemma. The first is to educate computer programmers and developers about the telephony world – and about the profit margins they can enjoy through being a successful CT developer. The second is to remove the need to understand the intricacies of the telephone world from by simplifying application development by using open architecture.

Whichever CTI application approach is used, the general benefits are similar. Clearly, CTI developers need to consider carefully which approach is right for the particular application they need to build. If the end requirement is a low cost, low-end stand-alone solution, then it's usually better to write code from scratch. However, as the solution gets more complicated (in particular if developers need to modify code at some point in the future) then the open architecture approach usually makes sense. Enhancements to open architecture can dramatically reduce the development time required to produce a given application, as well as provide developers with increased power and flexibility.

Toolkit vendors have also extended their product offerings to include complete, state-of-the-art applications known as plug-in-solutions. These range from telephony server applications to voice mail applications and IP telephony server systems.

Next generation toolkits are set to revolutionise the task of developing of building CTI applications. For the first time, computer programmers can look to develop call control and other telephony applications in the knowledge that they are working within a flexible and powerful environment – yet don't need to get involved in the detail of the telephone world. Contact centre, telecoms and IT managers also benefit from these more advanced solutions because they can more easily alter applications at a later date to take into account changing user requirements, incorporate moves, changes and so on.

A set of standard functions would be available, which would be pre-defined, to connect one system to another. The user could then integrate one or many external systems together in a far simpler way using common tools or commands. This makes the integration of multiple systems far easier and quicker.

- Graphical user interface – *the way in which the system administrator interacts or re-configures the systems has changed dramatically over the past ten to fifteen years. Originally system administrators would need to spend weeks training on the system probably learning a new language and finishing the course with an armful of documentation. On some systems individual programs would have to be loaded to make the simplest of changes. On others complex mnemonics would have to be memorised with strange error messages being returned after simply syntax errors. After wading through many books you would then realise that a comma had been mistakenly inputted instead of a full stop.*

This has all changed with the availability of graphical applications where the system administrator only needs to drop small icons around on a screen to completely reconfigure a system. Complex applications can be designed tested and implemented in days rather than many weeks or months.

Unfortunately there is a down side to this. Mistakes are easy to make and generally the changes are made almost immediately causing many problems within the contact centre environment. Calls suddenly being routed to the wrong group of advisers could route to a different site or even be routed into the ubiquitous 'black hole'. Care needs to be taken when using these applications as thousands of calls can suddenly disappear or appear in the most unexpected places.

- Flexibility – *not only has the software become more and more flexible the hardware has changed considerably too. Systems nowadays tend to be modular in their appearance and construction. In the past a hardware upgrade would require a small army of engineers to re-engineer a system due to expansion or upgrades. Systems would be out of service for many days with team working round the clock just to complete the work within the timescales. Problems would always mysteriously appear and many hours spent on the phone to the USA trying lots of different options hoping the next suggestion would work.*

Nowadays a single engineer can perform most upgrades that are now fully documented and have been performed many times over in the past. The circuit boards which provide the connections to the ACD can now fit in any available card slot whereas in the past only specific cards could be place in specific slots causing problems when none of the slots were available. Due to this modularity systems are more reliable particularly under high load conditions or large call volumes.

The disadvantages of the systems currently available are:

- Costs – modern call processing systems are a major investment within the contact centre environment. The more sophisticated the systems are, the more open their software and applications are greater the cost. Huge sums of money are spent developing the software to not only be flexible but also remain stable under load. As new applications or functionality is increased more often than not the manufacturer will price the software on the number of advisers on the system as opposed to a one off payment for an unlimited number of users. Some software will be sold for use by a concurrent used basis. The options nowadays vary from manufacturer to manufacturer and application by application, either way the software applications can cost as much, if not more, than the hardware in some cases.

- Support – for a medium-to-large contact centre the support required to maintain modern systems is proving to be an ever-growing problem. In the past the system administrator had limited access to the core operating software. CTI and IVR were available in a very limited form and management information systems gave basic information out. With the advent of open systems and accessibility to change the main system software, the support staff now have to be truly multi-disciplined. Voice and data are now converging with computer systems controlling the routing and handling of voice calls. Telephone systems can be reliant on large databases to enable successful call routing or completion and, with CTI, the delivery of simultaneous voice and data, the people required to support a modern contact centre need to have a sound background in both voice systems and data systems.

  This has proved difficult as traditionally people tended to train in one discipline or the other and never crossed over. Equally, manufacturers are finding it difficult to ensure all their field and support staff are kept up to date on the systems which they support and maintain. As software versions change as many as two or three times a year the costs and time in ensuring engineers are fully conversant in all aspects of the software are enormous. Even once all the training has been completed these inter-working problems need to be addressed between different software variants or hardware versions.

  Support staff need to understand, not only the complexities of call routing, but need expert knowledge on call management, IVR and CTI systems, voice recording and call monitoring systems. Larger organisations with multiple sites *also have to have voice and data network experts and the ability to run complex applications which produce consolidated reports regardless where calls are delivered to or answered.*

Large contact centre networks, which span continents, prove some of the hardest to support. Standards differ from country to country in respect to the way in which calls are delivered to the ACD, local expertise, country specific software and time differences. All these factors contribute to the overall problem of having the most suitable staff support, in some case, a company's main contact channel for its customers. The loss of any of the systems can cause the company many thousands of pounds per hour for each hour the system are down. If the main switching platform fails their customer cannot call in to order goods or services. If the management information systems fail then peaks and troughs in call traffic cannot be effectively handled, staffing levels cannot be monitored and overall performance to their customers cannot be maintained. Within a regulated environment, such as finance or insurance, the loss of the management information system or others such as voice recording could breach their operation licence and the ability to continue to service the incoming calls.

- *Depreciation – we have already covered the vast sums of money invested when setting up a contact centre. One of the big problems is how soon the current technology becomes out of date and the initial capital expenditure soon decrepitates to the point where, in some cases, it is more cost effective to re-new a system rather than upgrade it.*

As with modern personal computers, ACD systems utilise the same core components. Processors have become faster and faster, hard drives are now bigger than ever and the cost of memory have stabilised to an extremely affordable price.

All these factors contribute to depreciation. No sooner has one version of software been launched then the next version with greater functionality and features is just around the corner. In the past huge external hard disc arrays would be required to store the mountains of information. As technology progresses storage devices are tiny compared to ten or 15 years ago.

It has not been unknown for contact centres who have spent many millions of pounds on state of the art systems to find themselves in a position three or four years later looking to replace them due to technological advances and market forces.

Modern contact centres want to provide the best services available to meet its customers' demands and to ensure it is providing the same, if not better, services than its competitors are providing. ACD systems bought some years ago may not be able to cost effectively deliver the voice applications which customers have now come to expect. IVR systems and multimedia centres are now considered the norm and customers now enjoy these services. However, from a contact centre point of view a major overhaul of its systems may have been necessary to deliver these services. Although, in some cases, these IVR and CTI may go some way to reducing the overall head count, a large investment would have had to have been made initially to enable the systems to cater with these new applications.

2.1.5 *The criteria for choice for the contact centre manager*

Modern contact centre mangers have an extremely varied choice as to the type of systems available to them. From switching platforms to management information (MI), voice recording, wallboards, IVR and CTI platforms, performance monitoring, resource planning, powerdiallers . . . the list is endless.

The questions contact centre managers would have to ask themselves are regarding the operation of the centre. Is the contact centre:

- *primarily inbound or outbound?*
- *purely a contact centre environment or a mixture of front and back office?*
- *standalone or networked?*
- *Who are the type of customers and what market it will operate in?*

Once these questions have been answered then a contact centre manager will have a better idea as to the type and complexity of functionality they need. Most contact centres, regardless of operation, would require the best call management information (MI) available; this is probably the most important factor to consider. The ability to manipulate the data and present it in the most appropriate way will be extremely important.

Contact centres wishing to deliver advanced voice applications will need a platform that supports open standard API's to swiftly deliver them with little effort or support. A primary outbound contact centre would look for a robust a stable power dialler capable of processing thousands of call per hour.

Many contact centre managers prefer large colourful wallboards displaying real time statistics on call flows and agent availability or performance; others would use discreet applications running on the adviser's computer to display similar information.

Most modern contact centres would make use of call monitoring equipment in conjunction with voice and data recording. These systems provide valuable information on how advisers perform, the quality of each call and methods of improving processes or scripting. Contact centre managers can, historically or in real time, listen and view what individual advisers are doing from their own computer. They can replay the entire call, watch which screens agents used and the data they inputted. Those contact centres which only have voice recording facilities, managers once again use a system for quality monitoring, customer complaints and individual staff training.

Even the basic ACD provides a variety of sophisticated routing, queuing, and management features. Advisers in an ACD environment are generally assigned to a queue, which is a group of advisers handling the same type of calls. Basic ACD features can be assigned by queue to meet the different needs of diverse adviser groups. A telephone number can be linked to an ACD queue by associating a published number, often a 0800 or 0870 number. The basic ACD Call Centre options offer many important applications, discussed below.

Flexible routing – choose how incoming calls should be routed to advisers within a queue. Calls can be routed to the first available adviser or to the most-idle adviser – in a single queue or across all queues within the contact centre. When all advisers are busy, calls can overflow to alternate locations.

Queuing options – if no adviser is available, the ACD queues incoming calls. While in a queue, callers can be connected to an announcement, and then to music to let the caller know the call has not been dropped. A priority queuing feature could allow the designation of important calls as priority. Calls that have been in queue beyond the time interval set for the queue can be redirected to an alternative destination. This ensures the number of abandoned calls is kept at a minimum.

Call work codes –during or after the call, the adviser can enter a string of digits and send these digits to the Management Information system for management reporting. Managers can use this information to analyse contact centre productivity, adviser performance, or marketing campaign success.

Reason codes advisers can be required or requested to enter one of a number of numeric identifiers when they change to the 'auxiliary work' or 'after call work' mode or when they log out, in order to indicate the reason for the change in state. The tracking and reporting allows managers to understand more fully the ways in which advisers are spending their time. With reason codes, managers can make better use of resources and plan staffing more efficiently.

Malicious call trace – this feature alerts the contact centre to emergency or threatening calls. The system gathers trace information and can connect a voice recorder to the call.

Statistic – real-time contact centre statistics are displayed on voice terminals and wallboards. Empowered advisers can watch their own progress and make decisions based on contact centre conditions. Supervisors and managers can also monitor the progress of each of their advisers, adviser groups, applications, and trunk groups.

2.2
Explain the growth of management information systems

Management information (MI) has developed over the last 40 years with the growth in information-based roles such as those in the service sector and the growth in the sophistication of technology. The purpose of management information systems is to improve the performance of people in organisations through the use of information technology. The focus should be the people who make up the organisation as they affect the performance of the organisation as a whole. There will always be issues around how to define and measure performance however there is a need to maximise the technology available to do this.

The management of modern contact centres is totally reliant on the supply of information regarding the number of calls being delivered to the contact centre, the time they arrive and duration. The need to know how the advisers are performing, how many advisers are required on any particular shift, etc, is important. With the use of a management information system (MIS) the contact centre manager can use this information to ensure staffing levels are appropriate to meet the daily call patterns. They can also identify training needs through monitoring agent performance and the overall service level or percentage of calls answered (PCA) is achieved.

In managing the performance of the advisers and the centre typical questions that contact centre managers will be concerned with are as follows.

- *How many calls are being handled?*
- *How many callers hang up before talking with an adviser?*
- *How long are callers willing to wait for an adviser?*
- *How are advisers spending their time?*
- *Is the adviser workload being fairly distributed among all adviser queues?*
- *Do we need more trunks?*
- *How has traffic changed in a given ACD split over the past year?*

Some of these questions are far more important to the actual running of the contact centre than others.

Question

Which question occurs the most frequently amongst centre managers?

Probably the most commonly asked question by contact centre managers is 'how long are callers willing to wait?'.

As the technology becomes even more sophisticated then the amount of data that can be collected and analysed will increase. This should not however be at the detriment of the people who actually undertake the work itself.

2.2.1 Explain the role of information in the decision-making process

Information is the key element in the design, operation and performance of any contact centre. The more information gathered from customers, ACD systems and in house systems, the better able it is to forecast call trends, market trends or sales figures and ultimately the easier it is to manage the effects of these trends. This information helps users to reach decisions; the MIS does not make the decision for the user. The users themselves have to engage their experience and judgment to help them. Users can view the information as a series of charts (bar and pie charts), time series charts (graphs where one axis is over time), hierarchy charts showing organisational structures, sequence charts such as flow charts or even motion graphics for very sophisticated applications. Viewing pictorial representation of information can be much easier to spot the trends hidden within it.

With all this data the systems which collect it need to be powerful enough to handle inputs from multiple sources and have the storage capacity the provide historic or real data. With new storage mediums such as compact disc or optical disc the storage devices have greatly reduced in size enabling even more data to be stored for greater periods of time. In the past a standard floppy disc contained 1.4 Mb of information; with the advent of compact discs this increased to 650 Mb and optical or Digital Versatile discs have increased this even further. This means that the data can be stored for greater periods of time ready to be analysed to ensure a pattern of calls or trends can be tracked over previous months or years enabling the contact centre managers to ensure these trends can be met.

2.2.2 Describe the types and sources of information

Management information systems are now as important as the switching platforms themselves. Information is important on the volume of calls and performance of agents but there are other sources of data, which are just as important. Inevitably contact centres will have a large database relating to its current customers and a database relating to products or services it is providing.

The customer database is very powerful and can be used to the benefit of the company to target specific geographical, economic or social needs. Companies can also use this information to up-sell products to specific customers effectively. An example of this may be a company selling financial services and insurance services. If a client calls to make an enquiry regarding a financial services product, once the adviser knew who the caller was and where they lived, they could up-sell the caller home insurance using an external database which provided the caller with information on high crime rates in a particular geographical area. This demonstrates how a simple policy or product enquiry has generated further revenue for the company by simply understanding where someone lives and a piece of information that can be used as a lever to create the up-sell.

Question

What basic information is held on your customer's data records?

The basic information held on each customer, probably looks something like this:

- *first name;*
- *last name;*
- *salutation;*
- *mame tag/first name;*

- *mailing address;*
- *daytime telephone;*
- *evening telephone;*
- *fax;*
- *e-mail address;*
- *ethnicity;*
- *date entered into system;*
- *date information was last updated;*
- *affiliation/agency/company;*
- *referred by;*
- *contribution(s) (include date); and*
- *participation category/ies (events attended/project involvement/etc).*

Each of these categories can be used to target specific customers for products and services. Additional information will be held regarding products that customers have bought and services they have contracted into. This information is known as primary data, i.e. it has been collected by the organisation itself. Information collected by a third-party is known as secondary data, such as the data on crime rates for specific geographic areas for the example above.

Companies have their own internal databases that are equally as important to retain existing customers. These databases are nowadays of open architecture, such as Oracle, and enable a whole range of different software applications to access this common data source and manipulate or present the information in whichever manner the end user wants. This could be to segment customers into different groups depending on their account profile or product holdings.

Using a software application for call data, the information is generally presented in either a tabular or graphical form showing a whole array of customer or call information as described in section 2.1.5.

2.2.3 *Demonstrate an understanding and use of management information*

Management information, as previously explained, is a crucial element within the contact centre environment. This information is held in a common database the structure if which is generally described as a matrix or array. Along the top of the matrix are reference points or fields. These contain specific information, in customer information, such as first name, surname or date of birth. Entries or records are entered with the information in the relevant fields. The following table represents a simple database structure.

Fields

First name	Surname	DOB	Account number	Contact number	Address

Records

Records are added for each customer or contact. The number of fields is virtually unlimited although to make them easier to use a restriction is usually set whilst the database is being formed. Searches are then made across the database by using one of the fields as a reference point and search across that reference point with a known piece of information. For example if you knew a customers account number, using the above example, you would use 'Account No' as the reference point and search through all the account numbers until a match was found. If a match is found then all the information on that line or record will be associated with that account number. If no match were found then a return or error code would be given back.

The above table shows the structure of a simple customer database. An operational database for a contact centre would contain date, time, duration, abandoned, queuing time of calls and information regarding the adviser such as total time taking incoming calls, making outgoing calls, how long in idle or wrap and any wrap up or after call codes. Once again searches can be made across that database for specific events or groups of events such as how many call were taken on a specific day or time or agent.

Research shows that customers expect their calls to be answered within five to seven rings. There are several questions that need to be posed to those whose calls are not answered within that period.

Any call analyst will tell you that, whilst the contact centre adheres to its industry benchmark service level of 80% of calls answered in 20 seconds, the remaining customers are destined to wait in queue for any amount of time.

Consider the following scenario where a contact centre is handling 360 six-minute calls per hour. Using 'Erlang C' (the basic contact centre queuing formula) the calls would be handled by 42 agents at 100% occupancy to achieve the desired service requirements. However, in just meeting the target there will always be some customers waiting, due to the nature of random events linked to the arrival of the calls. In this example, for all calls not achieving the goal there is, on average, a 60-second wait with 10% of all customers left in queue longer than one minute (see Table 1). Service levels set as key performance parameters, within which the staffing is balanced, have condemned customers to holding!

Abandoned call rates immediately tell you when customers hang up and where in the queue they have hung up but it is almost impossible to evaluate how many of them call back. Caller line identification (CLI) can provide some statistics on repeat numbers that have called but calling from the office or from home will cloud the validity of the statistics. A realistic picture of how many customers call as opposed to how many calls are offered can only be achieved by answering 100% of all calls.

The quality of the queue message is directly related to call handling service levels. The quality of the message will impact on the callers' behaviour. An effective set of messages will increase the patience of customers so that they will be willing to hold until they are answered.

A poor set of messages will increase the propensity of the customer to hang up and either call back later or call an alternative provider. Table 1 shows the three extreme scenarios demonstrating this relationship.

Table 1 Extreme scenarios demonstrating the relationship between customers, queues and call centre measurements

No of customers calling	% (and no.) of customers going to queue	Quality of set of queue messages	Customer's response	Total calls offered	Total calls handled	% call abandoned rate
10,000	20 (2,000)	Good	Hold until answered	10,000	10,000	0
10,000	20 (2,000)	Poor	Hang up and call back later	12,000	10,000	17
10,000	20 (2,000)	Poor	Hang up and call an alternative provider	10,000	8,000	20

Organisations can try to stem the problem at source by providing freephone numbers to highlight their commitment to customer service and not charge customers for holding. The value is very quickly lost if the wait is too long.

Another option is to improve the staffing parameters and set service levels of 90% of calls answered in ten seconds, and in the above scenario an additional three staff at 100% occupancy would be required. The analyst would point out that 10% of customers will wait on average 40 seconds with 3% of all calls waiting for over a minute. The problem has been reduced though not eradicated.

Many studies have looked at the changing attitude of customers to holding and the different options currently being provided whilst on hold. Their first rule is simple: answer the call within three rings; the second rule was inconclusive, showing customer preferences fluctuating across all the techniques, eg, music, company or product information, ringing, engaged tone, information on the queue and information on where they are in the queue.

The only technique that interacts with the customer is the intelligent queue that announces the position of the customer in the queue. None of the other techniques are able to create this feeling of involvement. They are only able to appease or delay the feeling of frustration.

In a 1994 study, 54% of all customers preferred the intelligent queue because customers perceived that they had been recognised and that they were already involved in the engagement process. This preference rapidly diminished because there was not enough information to accurately predict when the call would be answered because it could not say how many staff were in and what the average call duration was.

The ultimate goal of any queuing system is to manage and enhance the customer's involvement with the company. Several recent surveys have shown there is no single right answer for what should be used in a queuing system; no single piece of music, or rings, or information source will create the right environment to suit all customer types. Proactive use of a combination of the techniques according to the information known about the caller can start to create the aura of involvement.

The queue content can be assimilated to the customer profile and the reason for calling by differentiating between prospects, first time callers, ordinary and premium customers and also differentiating between the call content: service, sales or enquiry. For example, first-time callers could be informed of the website and it's functionality, whilst existing customers could be informed of new services offered by the web. Callers could be told information, which is beneficial or interesting to their own circumstances and, at the same time, promote the brand in a manner consistent with the corporate image.

Call queues need not be seen as an unfortunate but necessary evil of call flow dynamics where brand image and customer service is ignored. The quality of the queuing system is an integral part of the customer contact strategy. It requires significant resource to examine how it can be developed to subsequently improve some of the related key performance measurements such as abandoned and answered rates.

Question

What can you do to address the queuing issue?

There are a few actions that can be undertaken to address the queuing issue.

- *Measure the number of your customers who have to wait and how long they wait.*
- *Examine variance and maximum wait-time, not just the average.*
- *Estimate how many of your customers are calling back and how many never call again.*
- *Consider how much business is lost through abandoned calls and how important your abandoned rate is to senior management.*
- *Qualify the effects the queue has on brand image and the qualitative factors of the call.*
- *Create workshops with customer service advisers, customers, marketing, and management to try and measure the qualitative factors.*
- *Examine your options, given your resource constraints.*
- *Understand the tools and techniques currently available to assist with the queuing message.*

If you can make your customers want to wait, both quantitative and qualitative benefits will be achieved in your performance measurements.

There are practical things to do with your queue, as follows.

- *A recent survey found that callers hold for an average 33% longer if they are listening to music rather than voice – callers hearing a voice message waited for three minutes before hanging up, while those hearing music waited, on average, for four minutes.*
- *Choosing the right music is important. Music should suit the company/brand image or suit the customer profile. The trend is moving away from classical*

through to pop. However, companies are increasingly composing their own unique, original music.

- *Phonographic Performance Limited (PPL) licences the use of music for public recordings.*

- *Regularly review message-on-hold material to see what is happening in the marketplace and what your customers like.*

- *Change the message content regularly – depending on number of contacts per customer – experiment with different messages/music – change every four weeks to reduce repetition.*

- *For brand image, use a consistent voice – male or female or combination, but make sure it is consistent.*

- *Don't apologise! Saying 'Sorry all our advisers are busy' doesn't build a good brand image or keep customers holding.*

- *Prepare the customer – if customers need their pin number and a pen, you can tell them whilst they are on hold.*

- *Offer information about the service – but don't hard sell! Give information that is relevant and useful.*

- *Smart queue: 'You have approximately two minutes to wait' makes the queue 'visible' and allows the customer to feel they are nearing the head of the queue. However, if the caller waits longer than the time advised, more frustration is probably caused.*

- *Queue jockey 'you are third in the queue' gives people a better idea of where they are, but this can go badly wrong. If you have programmed in parameters giving VIPs or sales calls higher priority, callers can be third in queue then slip back to fifth in queue.*

It is important to note that in a typical contact centre, only five per cent of the total costs are for the technology. Money spent on salaries, network costs, and overheads account for more than 95 per cent of total operating expense.

> **Question**
>
> What are the benefits of having information obtained by the management information system?

The information obtained by using a management information system enables call centres to:

- *maximise call centre productivity and control expenses;*
- *forecast and plan for seasonal variations based on historical data;*
- *measure the effectiveness of marketing programs and plan new ones;*
- *reward and retain skilled advisers; and*
- *measure and improve service levels.*

Unit 3

Marketing in the Contact Centre Environment

3.1
Describe the concept of marketing and how it relates to contact centres

The majority of companies need and want to grow and increase their business. To do this most companies will need to invest in some form of marketing. Marketing is not just another name for selling, although selling does form part of the marketing activity. As we shall see marketing is both a business 'function' (many organisations have departments that look after marketing activity for the organisation) and it is also a business 'philosophy'. This means that it permeates all aspects of the business so making the customer the focus of what they do. There needs to be a shift from inward looking policies to outward looking customer focus. It is important that concern and responsibility for marketing reaches all parts of the organisation. Let us now look at what marketing is.

3.1.1 What is marketing?

There are many definitions for marketing and the word marketing can be used in many different ways and many different things.

Kotler, a leading American on marketing, said that marketing is: 'Human activity directed at satisfying needs and wants through exchange processes'.

This definition shows the requirement for work and formal activity, to give what people need and want from the product or service, and 'exchange' implies that there is a transaction of some sort taking place.

Think

> How does your organisation satisfy customers' needs and wants?
> What sort of 'exchange' takes place?

The definition from The Chartered Institute of Marketing is: 'The management process responsible for identifying, anticipating and satisfying customer requirements profitably'.

This puts responsibility for marketing onto the management team to ensure that this key activity is undertaken. It also highlights the need for profitability, which is an important requirement for commercial organisations, as without profits these organisations will fail.

The management process of marketing is therefore about ensuring customers receive:

- *the right information about the product;*
- *the right product or service and at a time and place that is convenient to the customer; and*
- *post-purchase satisfaction and that customers will want to buy from the organisation again*

Think

> How in your role can you contribute to providing customers with these things?

The role of the marketing function therefore is to support the management team in:

- *identifying customer needs and market opportunities;*
- *looking at how these customers can be grouped together in 'segments' (groups of people with similar wants and needs, e.g. young adults, the retired);*
- *looking at ways of making products and services attractive to these segments; and*
- *deciding upon the most profitable product, pricing, promotion, people and distribution strategies.*

Marketing could therefore be described as a matching process. Matching the capabilities of the company with the needs and wants of the customer. Simply put, it's about identifying customer needs, satisfying customer needs and making a profit for the company.

To ensure that there is no confusion between marketing and selling, selling is about communicating the features and benefits of the product or service to the potential customers. Selling will lead the customer through the buying process and lead to closing the sale. Selling involves persuading the customer to buy existing products. Marketing starts off by looking at customers' needs both present and future and then developing products and services to meet those needs profitably.

Think

What part of your role involves selling?

The marketing process in most successful organisations follows a planned process. Figure 3.1 shows a simplified flowchart containing the key elements.

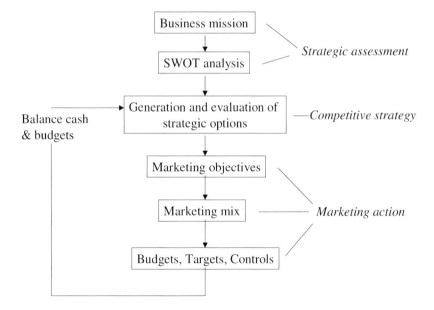

Figure 3.1 *The Marketing Planning process*

Think

> What is your organisation's business mission?
> How does your organisation intend to achieve its goals?

Many organisations have a high-level business mission, which is communicated to staff and customers. These tend to be quite broad and without measure e.g. 'To be the best retail bank in the world'. However the external business environment is ever changing and these statements need to be reviewed and amended over time. One way for organisations to do this is to do a 'SWOT' analysis. In this organisations to look at themselves and the products and services to they offer and how the external environment is likely to affect their business. SWOT is an abbreviated for strengths, weaknesses, opportunities, and threats. The SWOT analysis is a simple concept yet effective and valuable. By carrying out a SWOT analysis companies can create a simple structured way to think strategically. To complete a SWOT successfully, companies have to be objective and realistic.

So what does should the SWOT analysis include?

S – *Strengths of the company. This could include special, unique products or a first class level of service through attracting the best staff.*

W – *Weaknesses of the company. This could include poor management skills or products which are uncompetitive.*

O – *Opportunities outside of the company. This could include identified gaps in the market place through the advent of new technology.*

T – *Threats from outside of the company. This could include market trends or aggressive competitors.*

Strengths and weaknesses therefore look at internal factors within the company.

Opportunities and threats look at the external situation of the company. It may be that the organisation may wish to use external research to provide them with this information.

In the company		Outside the company (environment)	
Strengths	+	Opportunities	+
Weaknesses	–	Threats	–

Having carried out a SWOT analysis companies then need to compare the strengths with opportunities in the market and compare threats with weaknesses. It is possible that a company has the strengths to take on some of the opportunities available.

Equally the SWOT analysis can flag up an important opportunity that may have a corresponding weakness in need of addressing. This activity may also highlight some areas of competitive advantage for the organisation.

Carried out properly SWOT analysis can help companies place themselves in a better position to make strategic decisions based on information, which reduces risk in decision-making process. Companies should therefore bear in mind that a threat could turn into an opportunity.

Once the SWOT analysis has been completed it will then be translated into marketing objectives. These objectives will form the business plans for each of the operating units of the business. There needs to be cohesion between the plans to ensure that all the components of the organisation are pulling together. For example, imagine that, due to changes in tax legislation, the marketing department had devised a new form of savings account and they have forecasted that 50,000 accounts would be opened in the first six months of launch. The contact centre dealing with these enquiries about these accounts and the back office processing account opening would need to be ready to cope with this number of new customers, on top of servicing the existing customer base. That equates to, on average 1,923 new accounts each week.

Question

What would have to be put in place to deal with this increase in business?

Operationally there would be a lot to think about:

- *Is there enough capacity from the people already employed to deal with this increase. If not how many would need to be employed? What training will everyone need?*
- *Is there sufficient office space to accommodate new employees? What will their technology requirements be? Can the computer and telephony system cope with this?*
- *How does the product fit with other savings accounts? Will existing customers want to swap over? Should there be a fast track method for these existing customers?*

- *What interest rate should be offered to make it competitive yet profitable?*
- *What advertising and promotional activity will be undertaken? How will staff be involved in this? How should staff deal with enquiries?*

All these questions form part of the 'marketing mix'. The marketing mix includes such areas as:

- Product – *a means of solving a problem in the market, either an opportunity or a threat. In the financial services sector products are easily copied and a competitive advantage cannot be maintained for long through the product;*
- Price – *deciding on the right price for a product or service is essential. When setting prices companies need to consider:*
  1. *Is there any competition, if so what is the cost for the same or similar products or services on sale by competitors?*
  2. *Will the product or service be seen by customers as the best available to suit their needs?*
  3. *How much will it actually cost to produce the product?*
  4. *What profit margins are required to cover the costs of development of the product?*

  Price is a balance between the company and what it wants to sell the product for and what the customer is willing to pay.
- Place or Distribution – *is concerned with the selection of the most suitable form of distribution of a product. It can be about physically providing the goods to a customer, through shops or by post for instance, or about how the customer accesses services as in the contact centre environment. There are several factors which are important:*
  1. *Convenience and suitability. The chosen method of transport or access must be appropriate to the type of product or service;*
  2. *Products and services must reach the customer as quickly as possible;*
- Promotion – *is the art of informing and persuading customers to buy products. The idea behind the promotional element of the marketing mix is to move potential customers through the buying process. This means moving them forward from a state of unawareness to awareness, into understanding to feeling confident about the product or service, and ultimately to buying the it. The promotion mix is made up of several promotion tools such as advertising, personal selling, sales promotion and publicity. To ensure a successful promotion mix, companies need to contemplate which method to choose for promoting their product as well as selecting a suitable mode of media, such as television, national or regional newspaper, radio or direct mail, if necessary; and*
- People – *are very important in the marketing mix. This means that all employees*

of the organisation need to be constantly aware of how they can add value to the marketing effort. This is even more important in the contact centre environment where the advisers are the one point of contact for the customers they interact with.

For any company whatever the business or industry, it needs to remain customer focused. At the end of the day, without customers the company would not exist. To remain in business the needs and wants of the customer has to be a priority, whether it an existing or potential customer.

The budgets, targets and controls cascade through the organisation to team and individual level. A well thought out organisational business plan should be the sum of all the employees' performance appraisal targets who belong to the organisation. Individuals should be able to see where they contribute to the success of the organisation.

Think

How does your performance appraisal targets contribute to the success of your organisation?

3.1.2 *Difference between marketing strategies*

For any company to get to the position of marketing any product/service as we have seen it must have a plan. This is normally called a marketing strategy. There needs to be recognition in this strategy of the importance of competitors and customers in this strategy. The following are some examples of what can happen in practice:

- Self centred – *these types of organisations do not focus on the external environment of customers and competitors and constantly look at internal measures as the benchmark of success. These types of organisations do not compare their results with other peer group organisations or ask customers about their products or service;*
- Competitor centred – *these types of organisations obviously focus on their competitors' activity and ignore the needs of their customers;*
- Customer orientated – *here much attention is paid to the customers which is good, however, the competition may have ways of reaching these customers for more quickly and effectively; and*
- Market driven – *here the needs of the customer are balanced against how the competition can meet the needs of the customer*

Think

> Which of these strategies does your organisation pursue?

Another way of determining a strategy is by considering what competitive advantage the organisation has and how able it is to deliver it, i.e. what scope it has to do so. The organisation can attempt to be a:

- Cost leader – *this means that the organisation offers a low cost product or service to a large number of people, e.g. some of the low cost supermarkets follow this strategy;*
- Differentiator – *this may mean a higher price however the product or service is sufficiently different for everyone to want it, e.g. the next Harry Potter film. To be effective over the long term this product or service must be difficult to copy; or*
- Focus – *this is where the target market is much smaller and the focus can either be on cost or differentiation such as services to first time home buyers (cost of product) or wealthy investors (differentiation of service).*

By not actively pursuing a clear strategy the organisation can become effectively 'stuck in the middle' and in trying to be all things to all people can ultimately fail.

3.1.3 *Identify recent marketing trends*

There have been a number of trends in the last five years which organisations have been able to take advantage of in their marketing activities. Perhaps the biggest of this is the Internet, providing new ways for companies to reach customers and for customers to find out information about companies and their products and services. Many companies, however small, will have a website and this enables organisations to make far more information available and accessible at a fraction of the cost of printed brochures and postage.

This development has also allowed organisations to re-personalise they way in which they deal with their customers. Customers can be sent relevant information to them at their computer desk based on what they have previously bought via the website. Another spin-off from websites and personalisation has been delivery to the customer's door. Supermarkets have taken advantage of this re-introducing home delivery, which used to be the domain of the local shopkeeper. For a nominal fee the customer can sit at home and order their groceries from the website and receive them at home without having to go out to the shops. With improved physical distribution and delivery services many organisations have taken advantage of this from books, to flowers, to food even holidays and hotels in foreign countries. The list is endless.

This new distribution channel has helped contact centres to grow as a delivery channel and to take advantage of many of the other technological developments that have already occurred (See Unit 1). Added to this is the fact that customers are becoming more sophisticated and taking up new innovations more quickly. For example DVDs replacing video have been taken up twice as quickly as CDs were when they replaced vinyl disks. This means that organisations can be more confident when launching new innovative products that the consumers will be ready to buy them.

3.1.4 How marketing works in the contact centre environment and the differences between marketing products and services

So what does all this mean for contact centre operations and in particular those in the financial services industry? First and foremost the objective for any contact centre is handle customer enquiries effectively. This should be through an even distribution of calls and easy access to other departments and areas of the company. Contact centres need the ability to monitor the effectiveness of the service they provide. The fundamental objectives should be to differentiate the company on the basis of customer service as well as increase revenue and profit. These high level targets will probably be handed to the contact centre from the head office outlining organisational objectives to be achieved.

For general day-to-day servicing of customer needs, contact centres need a basic level of call handling capability. This will include basic queuing, agent reporting and delay and hold requirements, and when a contact centre moves into the realms of running marketing campaigns, it is vital that it has the ability to generate and handle the volume it expects to ensure it is well managed. It can be at this point that the problems start emerging. Contact centre advisers may be faced with complaints from customers. These complaints are normally generated because the customer has waited too long for his call to be answered. Advisers themselves will complain to their supervisors because the work is not being equally shared or that covering calls during breaks is impossible. These are classic problems that contact centres run into. Customers will of course wait, but for how long? Advisers want to be treated fairly and handling the load can sometimes conflict with other duties and requirements. For a contact centre to succeed and move forward, issues such as these should not be overlooked or underestimated. It is highly likely that the existing telephone system could cope quite adequately with the volume of calls and the amount of advisers, however changes would need to be implemented, with the objective to do better with the available resources. Features and functions that allow better use of advisers and information on how the contact centre and its advisers are performing need to be explored.

So before contemplating any running sales campaigns, a contact centre should look at the general goals and objectives involved.

Question

What goals and objectives should be put in place prior to running a sales campaign?

The following objectives should be considered before running a sales campaign.

- Grade of service. *How long will the calling customer wait before being handled by the call centre? This can be measured in a number of ways, however the most popular types are average speed of answer, average delay, longest delay, abandonment rate and percentage of calls handled in 'n' seconds.*

- Talk time. *Can the length of the average transaction be reduced? Generally, if this is possible all other operating statistics will improve.*

- Expanding the caller's tolerance for delay. *Various methods are introduced by contact centre to convince the calling customer to wait longer than they would normally be willing to wait. Techniques normally employed include music-on-hold and playing frequent delay messages.*

- Agent wrap-up time. *Reducing or eliminating the after call work for advisers has the same operational effect as that of reducing talk time. A wrap-up code is usually entered at the end of a call to identify the type of call the adviser has just taken.*

- Call load. *By identifying why customers are calling may result in a reduction of the number of calling customers that need to speak to an adviser direct. Are callers asking for the same information, if so can these callers be handled by an automated service?*

As a contact centre evolves, the way in which it handles calls will change and in turn will become more complex. Improvement in call handling will be required to decrease waiting time, the number of advisers will need to be matched to incoming call volume, adviser productivity will need to be improved to reduce call holding times, network resource will need to become more efficient and the general availability of the call centre increased.

So to ensure customers are satisfied and remain satisfied the optimum for a contact centre should be to have the ability to:

- *decrease waiting times for calling customers;*
- *decrease transaction times;*
- *handle large call volumes;*
- *continue to improve the quality of the call handling; and*
- *increase network reliability and contact centre availability.*

Fundamental to all this of course is the ability to continue offering a distinct service while maintaining an increase in revenue.

Having already established that marketing is based on meeting the needs and wants of customers, it is vital that companies develop products that are viable, i.e. products that satisfy these needs. A product plays an unquestionable role in the marketing process and it is therefore crucial for companies to determine, match and offer the right product to potential customers. Products are more than the tangible goods the customer buys. A product is a combination of the benefits it provides, tangible features and any additional services that may accompany it. Companies need to look at the core benefit the customer actually purchases when it buys a product. Then they need to look at the actual, physical components of the product – what is the quality of the product, what are its features, what is its brand name, how will it be styled and how will it be packaged. Finally, what additional service, if any can the company offer the customer, such as after sales service, warranty, delivery. By looking at products in this way, companies may identify areas of improvements and possibility gain advantage over their competitors.

Of course, not all companies sell a tangible product. More often than not companies within the financial services industry sell services. Developing a marketing strategy for services is somewhat different.

Question

How are services different from products?

Services have a number of unique features that need to be considered. Unlike a product a service is 'intangible', it cannot be seen, tasted, felt, heard or smelled. This in itself makes evaluating the service quality difficult and potential customers will look for other visible indicators of quality, most generally based on the experience they have in interacting with the company adviser or representative.

Services are produced and consumed at the same time and cannot therefore be separated from the provider, they are 'inseparable'. It is for this reason that the people involved become one of the most important factors when marketing services. Both the company and the customer must interact for the service to occur and therefore both parties become part of the service provided. As such, the actual quality of services may vary depending on who provides the services, when, where and how.

Services are consumed as they are provided and therefore cannot be stored for use later on, as such they are 'perishable'. Companies may encounter problems if demand fluctuates and service opportunities are missed. Strategies must be developed to ensure that demand is managed at a constant flow or that the company can continue to supply the service to meet the fluctuating demand.

Finally there is 'heterogeneity', or diversity. At first glance a bank account would appear to be identical to the next one, however, because the service is based on the experience the customer has in interacting with the organisation or their representative it will be very different and personal to them.

3.1.5 The importance of the customer in the marketing equation

Getting the balance right is therefore imperative to the marketing of any product or service. However, marketing is about keeping existing customers as well as acquiring new ones. To encourage business with customers both old and new, it is essential for companies to build and maintain good customer and supplier relationships.

To survive a company needs to ensure that its products and services remain attractive and continue to satisfy customer needs. Companies need to ensure that they move with the times, keeping up with the changing needs and demands of their customers. By communicating effectively with customers companies are placed in a better position to understand and ensure that their product/service is delivering what the customer wants and needs. Keeping in close contact with customers enables companies to observe and make improvements to their products and services to better satisfy their needs. This can be by listening to customers when they complain and acting on the nature of the complaints, conducting customer satisfaction surveys, holding customer focus groups to ask them questions about how they find the products and services the company offers or conducting independent research with the general public.

So, in the marketing equation customers are extremely important. Companies that ignore customers, ignore the customer loyalty that would effectively deliver future business and profit. Loyalty plays an important part in maintaining profits for companies. When customers feel that their needs are being catered for and valued, they are less inclined to look elsewhere. If customers are satisfied with the product/service they receive they are more willing to refer the product/service to others, creating new potential customers and ultimately profit. Customers are more inclined to spend more money with a company when they feel valued and that their needs and wants are considered and are likely to be less irritated by price increases.

The growth in number of happy, loyal customers can be a tremendous boost for any company and should never be underestimated or taken for granted.

Customer satisfaction is the only route to gaining a long-term sustainable competitive edge. Attracting and retaining customer loyalty is a major issue for each and every company.

3.2
Explain the ideas of customer markets, segmentation and buyer behaviour

This next section goes on to explain some common terms that are found in marketing. You will probably see that your central marketing function will undertake some of these activities and you see the result of that research and activity affecting how you interact with different customers or groups of customers and the types of products and services you can offer them.

3.2.1 How does the organisation define a customer market

After executing a SWOT analysis (as in section 3.1) the company will have established the internal strengths and weakness of the company and the external opportunities and threats that may exist. Part of this SWOT analysis will almost certainly be to define the different customer markets exist. This will then filter into the marketing objectives and what the organisation hopes to achieve.

So what does the term 'market' mean? The word 'market' actually refers to the place where buyers and sellers meet. The term market will usually be defined as 'all the possible buyers'. However, some companies will not want always want to 'target' all potential buyers. In fact, many potential buyers do not purchase immediately and in many cases some years after a product or service has been launched.

The organisation must therefore decide how it wishes to define the market. A market can be defined narrowly or broadly, the organisation can chose the parameters it uses to do this. When considering this, the organisation needs to bear in mind the resources available as well as its intended strategy. By defining broadly, the company will be marketing to a larger audience of actual and potential buyers. But it also means that the number of competitors will increase. Defining the market narrowly will produce the opposite effect.

Forecasting demand for a product or service is not as easy as it first seems, particularly if the product or service is completely unknown to the customer.

Question

What are the issues with forecasting demand?

Forecasting can be quite difficult and poses a number of difficult questions.

- *How can the number of customers be predicted and targeted for a product or service that is unknown?*
- *If the product or service is launched into an already established market, how will the competition react?*
- *What is the probability of other competitors joining the market in the future and what impact would that have?*
- *Customer preferences change, how will the launch of a new product affect the dynamics of that market?*
- *How stable will demand be once the product or service has been launched?*

Most companies will realise that their product/service cannot appeal to everyone within the market. Instead they must identify the 'segments' of the market that the product/service would best appeal. The company needs to decide which 'market-coverage' strategy it will use, and how it will segment and select the target market.

There are three types of market-coverage strategy available to companies. Undifferentiated, differentiated and concentrated.

When a company selects an 'undifferentiated' marketing strategy it would basically ignore difference between market segments and approach the market as a whole with just one offering. This approach is based on the common customer needs rather than what is different. It is intended to appeal to the largest number of customers. Undifferentiated marketing can be very beneficial and cost effective. However, the downside of this type of marketing is that it can be very difficult to produce a product or service that will satisfy a large number of people. An example of an undifferentiated product is tinned tomatoes, which is similar across brands.

Choosing a 'differentiated' marketing strategy allows a company to target and market a product or service in several segments with special offers for each. This type of marketing approach has become more popular and companies have seen much benefit from higher level of sales than in the undifferentiated market. The disadvantage however is that the increase in cost as the promotion has to be adjusted to fit the different segments, i.e. different types and styles of advertising. An example here would be Sunny Delight juice drinks that are targeted at children through television advertising.

A 'concentrated' marketing strategy can be very useful to a company with very limited resource. Companies choosing a concentrated marketing approach will focus on a large share of one or more smaller segments. This approach helps companies to gain a strong market position in the segment of their choice and provides a way forward for the future. An example might be a local butcher who advertises to people in his area through a local newspaper.

Careful consideration needs to be taken by companies when selecting which of these marketing strategies to adopt. Companies need to think about the company resources, product variability, product life cycle (whether a product is newly-launched or nearing the end of its marketable life), market variability and the marketing strategies of their competitors.

3.2.2 What is segmentation and how can customers be grouped in segments?

Following on from the last section 'market segmentation' is the division of a totally mixed market into groups with relatively similar needs. Every market can be divided into groups of people with similar characteristics. Segmentation is important, as customers have unique needs and wants. Companies thinking about introducing a marketing strategy should first understand the difference between a need and a want in order to satisfy customers.

Let us look first at the difference between a need and a want. A need is the basic force that motivates a person to do something (Perreault, 1996). The basic human need is a state of felt deprivation, the physical need for food and clothing for instance, a social need to belong and an individuals need for knowledge and self-expression. These are needs that need to be satisfied. A want is the form that a human need takes as shaped by culture and an individual's personality (Assael, 1995). So it can be said that a person wants an object that will satisfy their needs. For instance, everybody needs some kind of liquid; this need is part of the basic make-up of humans. Rather than satisfy this with just water people have learned to satisfy this need with coke or lemonade, a want created by their social environment and advertising.

Question

What factors can be used to segment customer markets?

There are three main segmentation variables, those based on the following.

- Customer profile. *Age, class, disposable income, family size or geographic location. People living in large towns will have different needs for welling boots than those people living in rural locations. This is the most popular form of segmentation and is quite often used in conjunction with other parameters within this type of segmentation. For example, a company may first divide the country into North, South, East and West and then look at the demographics of the customers in each region based on their age or income.*
- Lifestyle and personality. *Where an individual aspires to a brand image or wants to be a trendsetter for instance. This is one of the reasons why some products are promoted very successfully on brand image such as Nike, Levi or Mercedes and can command a high price as a result.*

Think

What brand or lifestyle do you associate yourself with?

- Behavioural – *benefits sought by a product; when it is bought, why it is bought, what it is used for and the consumers beliefs and perceptions of the product. Segmenting on a behavioural basis is probably the most important segmentation variable.*

Think

How does your organisation segment its customer base?

The databases that organisations hold containing customer data can be interrogated to discover many of the details of the customer profile so that different segments can be identified. Some of the lifestyle, personality and behavioural segmentation will be more difficult to assess from the type of information held about customers. This may not always be the case as certain organisations will know that a customer buys from them because of say lifestyle reasons – say Ikea or Habitat – or because there is a behavioural reason – Thornton's Chocolate know that they will make more sales at Christmas and Easter when it is traditional to give chocolate as a present.

3.2.3 What is buyer behaviour?

When making a purchase a customer is influenced by several factors, as follows.

- Personal. *An individual will relate a want or need to a product/service and will therefore make a purchase believing that it will satisfy them. An example would be that a loan would help them purchase the car they wanted. This is often referred to as a personal factor. Other personal factors could include how much money an individual will have left after paying their bills, or whether they are single or married, what their role in the family is and how many dependents they have.*
- Psychological. *This is based on a person's past experiences, beliefs and attitudes. In the car example a customer may think that a Ford is the best model of car because they have bought a Ford before and found it to be a reliable car. It is difficult to change attitudes so from a marketing perspective it is more desirable to design products or services that fit the attitudes.*
- Social. *Social factors play a huge part in persuading a customer to choose a particular product or service over another. Quite often a buyer is influenced by a friend or family member's preference for a particular product or service. In the car example the customer's friends may have told them that they think another make of car is more reliable so they may be swayed to trying this type.*

- Cultural – *Cultural factors such as what customers believe in influence what a customer will buy. Customer attitudes based around attitudes to religion, age, family and marriage affect the product or service people buy. It is the pressure exerted by society at large and fashion which influences people here. In the car example the customer may think that because they now have two children that an MPV type of car might be the right choice for them because they think that is more acceptable type of car to have for a family.*

Two people with the same need will go through the same process but may end up with two different products because of these factors that shape their behaviour. The customer will go through a decision process when considering the purchase. This decision process will vary in length depending on whether the customer is a 'deliberate' or 'compulsive' buyer. The customer may not make this decision alone and may be influenced by a number of people.

The process that a customer goes through when they buy is as in Figure 3.2:

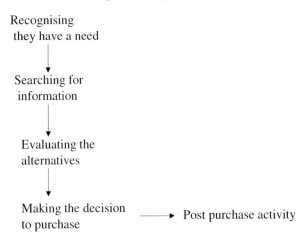

Figure 3.2 *The buying process*

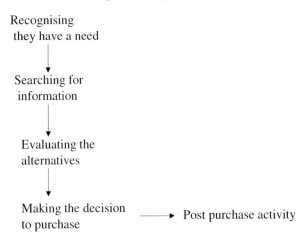

Question

Where do you search for information when you start thinking about making a large or important purchase?

You are most likely to look for help from those people close to you such as family, friends or colleagues, particularly if they have experience of the product when collecting information about a product you are considering buying. This is known as personal sources. You may look for general information from the press or specialist magazines – public sources. You may then look at the advertising or brochures of different companies who offer the product and even visit a showroom to talk to a salesperson. Whilst doing this you could try out the product – an experimental source. This information search will be very personal to you and will depend on your prior experience, whether you have bought the product before, the size, importance and complexity of the purchase – buying a tin of baked beans is not so important as buying a new house – and whether you have decided you want to try something different for a change.

Question

What factors do you take into consideration when you are comparing different products to purchase?

When comparing different products you will probably consider:

- *the product features such as its price, what it can do, its quality and styling;*
- *the relative of important of each of these features (for example when considering a new TV picture quality might be more important than the sound quality);*
- *your perception of each brand's image (for example Sony might be considered a better TV brand than Phillips); and*
- *how you intend to use each of the features and what the benefits are to you (so for someone who was hard of hearing and used the text facility when they watched TV the sound quality potentially would not really be of interest to them at all).*

These two stages are where organisations are able to influence the decisions that customers make and this will be looked at in more detail in the next section. Once the customer has evaluated the information they will make their decision and purchase the product. Once bought they will use and experience the product or service. This will then make a judgment against their expectations, which will affect their post purchase behaviour and feelings.

3.2.4 How buyer behaviour helps the organisation and the individual in their role

Although an organisation cannot directly control many of these influencing factors, it needs to understand the impact they can have. The organisation can then develop a marketing mix strategy that will appeal to the preferences of the target market. The following describes what organisations and individual employees can do to take advantage of each of the stages of the process.

- Need recognition. *The organisation should be aware of the current needs of its customers as well as insufficiently developed or insufficiently satisfied needs. In the case of services from financial services providers one of the prime reasons for customers to change providers is because they are dissatisfied with the levels of service they are receiving. Customer-facing employees are in a prime position to pinpoint unsatisfied customer needs from comments that may come out in conversations that they have with customers.*

- Information search. *As we have seen in the last section different purchases require different levels of information. Organisations can take advantage of this by putting information on their websites and making literature readily available to customers. Direct mail is a way of targeting certain customers with product information if it is likely to be relevant to them, however, this can be quite a costly exercise if not done in a focused way. Customer-facing employees can help customers with information by ensuring that they answer questions correctly and offer other information about the product or service that the customer may not be aware of. It is also important for staff to ask questions that will encourage the customer to discuss what their requirements are so the best match can be found.*

- Evaluation of alternatives and purchase decisions. *These parts of the process are where the customer goes to think about what they want to do and will probably not welcome intrusion at this point. However there would be no harm in the staff member making follow-up contact to check whether the customer required any more help before making a final decision.*

- Post purchase activity. *This is where good quality service is paramount. Depending on the way the customer has been treated during the buying process they will either recommend the organisation to their friends and buy a gain or take action that involves not buying again, telling their friends not to buy, making a complaint or, in the worst possible case, taking legal action. The organisation* can contribute to making customer service positive by having good systems and processes, for example, and the employees by being polite, friendly and undertaking actions they have promised the customer (see section 3.4). Doing this well will improve customer loyalty and increase the number of referrals of new customers made to the organisation.

3.3
State the importance of managing customer relations

In previous sections we explored the importance of the customer. This next section looks at managing customer relationships, why this is important and how this can be done. There is also a need to understand the differences between good and bad customer management and the impact on the parties involved.

3.3.1 Why managing the customer relationship is important for the customer, organisation and the employee

It is very costly for organisations to create new customers so therefore it is very important to ensure that the customer remains loyal. Therefore the ability to manage good customer relationships is vital for any company if it is to retain customers and to acquire new ones. If a good customer relationship does not exist or if the company chooses to ignore customer relations completely, the customer will not feel valued. This will result in the customer looking for a new supplier that can satisfy their needs. Eventually, the company will begin to lose customers, income and profit.

By creating good customer relationships companies will be able to rectify any issues or problems that may arise as well as learn of any preferences and/or dislikes customers have. So, employees need to be trained to listen to what the customer is actually saying. Listening to customers is an important skill that employees need to have in order to help not only the customer but the company too. Companies that make their customers feel valued are rewarded with profits. Customers are likely to remain loyal to the company that satisfies their needs and wants.

To create and manage good customer relations, companies need to offer the customer an efficient and effective service with before and after sales communication. A courtesy call is a good way of keeping the customer up-to-date, it is informal and can pre-empt any problems.

Creating a positive atmosphere with good communications will enable a company to resolve customer problems and issues efficiently and effectively. The company can then continue to offer the customer new products and services. Linking previous transactions and information collected about the customer will aid the rapport in the relationship. Organisations can build this functionality into the customer information that is available to advisers. When staff speak with them again, even though it may not be the person the customer spoke to last time, the adviser can ask how the holiday went (from knowing for example that foreign currency was ordered last time the customer called). Contact strategies can be built around identifying times to make proactive calls and offering different products and services from information collected about customers. These contact strategies can be different depending on the customer profile and what segment they belong to.

When staff interact with customers it is far more beneficial for both parties if this is done on a positive basis.

Question

What are the benefits to customer facing staff of a positive customer relationship?

For customer-facing staff the benefits are that they will gain job satisfaction, it is likely that the customer will say 'thank you' and respond in an appreciative way. The adviser will be less pressured and stressed and be looking forward to the next call. This will improve the adviser's confidence and encourage them to ask customers questions that could result in another service being taken up. This in turn will be good for team morale and improve income for the organisation, which should lead to better bonus prospects for the advisers.

3.3.2 Effective strategies for managing customer relationships and the role of the employee in this

Customer relationships must be continually worked at and built upon. Companies should aim to retain a lasting partnership with existing customers in addition to building relationships with new customers. Relationships can only continue when both parties, the company and the customer, communicate with each other. Communication is key to the success of any good long lasting customer relationship.

For good customer relationships to be maintained, companies need to ensure strategies are in place to cover all possibilities. Companies should start by setting standards for all employees and what acceptable levels of service are for customers. This may be in relation to dealing with complaints, responses to requests and certain scripts for telephone enquiries. Indeed, all personnel, no matter what their position or job within the company, must be educated about good communication and good customer relationships in order for these qualities to exist and be conveyed to the external customer.

Companies need to provide a punctual and efficient service to customers. By doing so, companies will give the customer the right impression, i.e. that the customer is really appreciated. If a customer is left in the dark without explanation when a service has not been provided or goods have not been delivered as promised, this leads to anger and frustration. A company that focuses on identifying problems that occur and dealing with them in an efficient and prompt manner will encourage and restore confidence and satisfaction in the customer. However, companies should not always have to learn from mistakes. They should carry out their own research and not simply wait until customers call with problems and complaints. By putting themselves in a customer's position, companies can identify and rectify any problems or issues before they arise. Customers are very valuable tools for providing information on the quality and efficiency a company's product/service. By offering customers the chance to voice their view either verbally or in a written survey, allows companies to identify difficulties or problem areas.

Good communication between a company and its employees is also essential. Without it employees are not likely to produce good or satisfactory results and they will struggle to work as a team. Job satisfaction will be low and employees will feel stressed. It is quite often the case that when employees do not feel appreciated they are not happy in their work and this is conveyed to the customer who in turn does not feel valued. Incentives for staff have become increasingly popular, as companies realise that if they are to keep good experienced people, these people need to be rewarded.

Individuals have an important role to play in the building and maintaining of customer relationships. The individual is in effect the crucial link in understanding both the internal and external customer. Individuals enable organisations to have a greater understanding and personal insight into the needs of the customer. It is, of course, the employees that are the face of the company and deal directly with customers. For employees to offer a good service to its customers, the employees must feel that they have the knowledge, skills and tools to do this. To be able to create good customer relations, a company must ensure employees are motivated and stay motivated too. The attitude of employees will be what comes across to customers irrespective of the individual employees ability to do their job.

Using the telephone, writing letters, sending e-mails and face-to-face interaction are all common forms of communicating with customers. Front line telecommunication is usually the first contact external customers have with a company. For customers this contact is very important – first impressions do count. Telephones are used extensively to develop business through telesales and telemarketing, as well as being an essential link between the company and the customer.

Customer complaints are one of the biggest opportunities that employees have of turning a negative experience of the organisation into a positive one.

Question

What can an employees do to turn round a customer complaint?

There are a number of things that employees can do to make this happen. Firstly listening carefully is vital if the customer is to be understood and dealt with appropriately and satisfactorily. Not listening will lead to misunderstandings and frustration and this could ultimately lead to a complete breakdown in the communication. Putting a customer at ease and having the ability to understand what is being said shows an appreciation of the customer's point of view. Being patient with the customer also allows the individual to accurately pinpoint and resolve any problems and issues. It is important to acknowledge problems that have occurred and apologise for them. Customers should always be reassured that problems will be dealt with and given a detailed explanation of how and when their problems or issues will be resolved. Customers should always be kept informed and up-to-date, particularly when problems or issues cannot be immediately resolved.

Another way in which individuals can build relationships with customers is by acknowledging information about the customer and building that into the conversation. Some technology enables advisers to see this information on screen as they talk and the adviser can make reference to this in their conversation. If for example has taken a loan for a new car the adviser can ask how the new car is going which will make the customer feel as if the individual is genuinely interested in them and more likely to remain loyal as a result. In this way it is easier for advisers to spot opportunities for cross-sales by improving their knowledge of the customer and their lifestyle.

Individuals are invaluable to any company and should never be underestimated in the management of customer relationships. Individuals are at the forefront of implementing and satisfying customer requirements.

3.3.3 How relationship management can go wrong and the effects on the organisation

Good relationships with customers can and do go wrong, and then turn sour.

Question

What can make a relationship go wrong?

There are a number of factors that can make a relationship go wrong:

- *communication is key to running any type of company and it is imperative that this does not stop. Not communicating can seriously damage any relationship whether built up over a short or long period of time. Frequently, relationship problems start because the needs or wants of a customer are not listened to;*
- *poor quality products or those that are not good value for money can damage the customer relationship. The company may pursue what the customer feels is an inappropriate policy, for example new customers are offered better deals on interest rates that are not available for existing customers to switch over to. This can badly affect customer loyalty, as the customer does not perceive that the company values their loyalty;*
- *where a customer receives bad service and actions the customer has asked to be done are not carried out;*
- *poorly trained staff or staff that have a poor attitude. Contact centres that present calls to advisers who do not have the correct skills will leave customers feeling annoyed and frustrated;*

- *where the technology or systems aren't sufficient to handle to volume and nature of enquiries leading to dropped calls and requests that cannot be dealt with;*
- *unresolved complaints and where staff are unable to reach a satisfactory conclusion with a customer where a problem has arisen; and*
- *external pressures such as poor media coverage can adversely affect an organisation where customers take their business away as a result.*

The effects of this are that customers lose confidence in the product or service and may feel rejected, unhappy and resentful. The result of which could ultimately be the loss or cancellation of custom and damaging the possibility of any future business. Over time the company image and reputation may be seriously damaged leading to loss of income and profit. This loss of customers reduces the amount of insight into how the product or service is performing and the organisation will not have the ability or have the opportunity to support or put right any problems or issues that may have occurred. Companies that choose not to communicate with their customer will not understand their needs or wants and cannot therefore help or support them.

3.3.4 The effect on the organisation of good customer relationship management

There a number of ways that good customer relationship can be maintained. For instance, an effective and efficient contact centre will ensure that advisers have the correct skill set to deal with calls that are presented to them. The result is that an adviser that has the right level of knowledge and experience deals with customers efficiently.

By offering and maintaining good relationships and good quality customer service, companies will see an increase in customer loyalty. Good quality customer service creates customer satisfaction and gives a company competitive advantage. Good relationships therefore benefit both the company and the customer.

When a company is concerned with keeping its reputation intact, good customer relationships and good communication must be a top priority. Customers that are satisfied with a product or service are generally happy with the company. By showing customers that they are valued and appreciated, companies build customer confidence. Customer confidence is essential if the customer is to continue to purchase products or services form that company that could quite easily be taken away by competitors willing and waiting to cater for their needs.

Customers that are satisfied with their purchase and the overall service provided by a company are more likely to buy again; and a satisfied customer is more likely to recommend the company to friends, family and work colleagues. Recommendation can improve a company's reputation and bring with it new customers and an increase in revenue and profit.

From an internal perspective, good relationships between company and employee will present itself to the customer. The employee will have an understanding of the kind of service they should be delivering because they themselves feel valued and appreciated.

A company that can prove to customers, that it has a reputation for good customer satisfaction and customer loyalty is a company that can enhance its chances of a long and profitable existence.

3.4
Describe the need for a quality culture in an organisation

Quality service is something that is regularly cited as something that all organisations strive for. Organisational cultures that promote this to customers are also something that many companies say they can offer. However what does this really mean?

Think

What does quality service mean to you?

There are various definitions of quality service such as:

- *meeting the stated requirements of the customer now and in the future;*
- *conforming to requirements or standards;*
- *it is about having the right attitude not just a process; and*
- *getting it right first time.*

Whichever definition you think is most appropriate it is only the customer who can judge the quality of the service that they receive.

3.4.1 *The need for a quality culture*

Some people are resistant to idea of a quality culture, they may prefer to keep their head down, get on with their own work and not to worry about others.

Question

Why do some members of staff behave in this way?

There can be a number of reasons why people behave in this way. They may perceive the customers to be a nuisance and that they should be grateful that someone is going to answer their query. They may think that the organisation has created problems for customers by the systems in place or the pricing policy. They may feel that their workload is such that they cannot do more than the bare minimum for each customer. Whatever their reasons this creates an unhappy environment in which staff morale tends to be low and there is an absence of teamwork.

Question

What are the benefits of creating a quality approach?

There are some distinct benefits of creating a quality culture. It can help a company turn an unhappy environment around by taking advantage of what each individual within the organisation can offer as a person. To achieve this, companies need to put in place a structured approach, so that all personnel can understand processes and procedures, which will help employees to create a teamwork atmosphere.

The saying 'we're all in this together', reminds us all that individual success depends on everyone working together. In the context of a company, it reminds employees that the company's success depends on the individual themselves doing their work well. To achieve this, employees must feel part of the bigger picture. Employees must be able to identify their own personal success within that bigger picture and understand that by working hard, they are achieving success not just for the company but for themselves too. This can be assisted by incentive schemes based on information collected about customer satisfaction levels.

3.4.2 Measuring quality

Measuring quality and customer satisfaction in the financial services sector is somewhat different and more difficult than in most other industries.

Think

Why is it difficult to measure service?

When we consider the services sector we include retailers, travel companies (airlines, train operators, buses, etc) hotels and so forth as well as the world of finance with its banking and insurance institutions. Therefore as a whole the services sector is very diverse and what may be right for one service may not be right for another even though they are within the same sector. As such the type of service provided can vary enormously.

Companies in other sectors or industries that either produce or sell goods are able to standardise methods, making it easy to measure the quality and saleability of goods by assessing the product itself. They can then make the necessary changes for improvement. It's so much easier for a company to measure quality against a tangible item – a product that a customer can buy and take with them.

In the financial services sector, the majority of services are intangible. The customer cannot physically take any 'product' home with them and check it over. Companies cannot check and inspect its services before selling it to the customer. The service is created with the involvement of the customer and therefore if there is no customer there is no service. Companies must therefore ensure that the customer is the focal point. Customer satisfaction is a good way for companies within the services sector to measure the quality of the service it offers.

Measuring quality will ensure that companies make improvements in the right areas. If companies do not measure quality, they will not know how well or how badly they are doing. For companies with the financial industry this means this means them ensuring that:

- *products and services offered meet the needs and requirements of its customers;*
- *customers are provided with sufficient information about available products and services;*
- *employees are knowledge and have adequate training on the products and services;*
- *employees have the ability to communicate effectively with customer;*
- *employees have been trained to deal effectively with customer queries, complaints and difficult situations;*
- *customers would recommend the product or service of the company to a friend; and*
- *levels of retention of customer accounts and numbers of new accounts being opened from recommendations are increasing (rather than decreasing)*

Question

So how does a company ensure customer satisfaction?

As previously mentioned, customers are key and their views and opinions on how well a company performs will differ because customers do not all come from the same background. Additionally, customer views will change from time-to-time depending on their experiences over a period of time. In a contact centre customer opinion will quite often be based on how an individual adviser handled the customer call, whether the adviser was knowledgeable enough on the products or service on offer or those of its competitors.

These are just some of the factors that make measuring quality within the sector difficult and subjective. The best way of finding out what satisfies customers is to ask them. One of the most effective ways of getting this information is by sending out questionnaires to customers analysing the feedback and then taking the necessary action.

Another way of measuring quality is to look at the number of complaints received from customers.

Question

How would you analyse information relating to complaints to check on quality of the service in your contact centre?

In a contact centre these areas and analysis could be around the following:

- *How many customer complaints were received within a month or quarter?*
- *What percentage were repeat complaints?*
- *What percentage of the complaints related to waiting time?*
- *What percentage of the complaints related to problems with Internet or system access?*
- *What percentage of the complaints related to system down-time?*
- *What percentage of the complaints related to the way the call was handled?*
- *What percentage of the complaints related to an employee?*
- *What percentage of the complaints related to transaction processing time?*
- *What percentage of the complaints related to overcharging?*
- *What percentage of the complaints related to incorrect debit transactions?*

Companies need to put in place a system that will ensure that they obtain feedback from customers on a regular basis and that this information is tracked. Then put in place suitable standards and procedures. For instance, a contact centre may set a standard stating that all incoming calls must be answered within three rings, or customer call backs must be made within four hours, or e-mail customer queries must be responded to within 24 hours.

Once standards and procedures have been made it is imperative for companies to continuously measure and monitor progress. Service quality control tables could be used to track progress, with any major divergence analysed and corrected promptly. Appropriate policies and procedures should be put in place to ensure quality of service is continuously improved.

3.4.3 *The issues with providing service and how individuals can contribute to this*

Employees need to recognise that a company is not just the building they work in with assets and other employees, but that it has customers. Employees who recognise this will understand that the good of the company is directly connected to that of its customers. Consistent success is the common goal for all parties. By employing this type of culture, employees can personally identify themselves with the company, showing concern for the welfare of other employees, the company and its customers.

Working in this way, will naturally help the development of teamwork and the promotion of people working together in teams to deal with tasks. It reminds people that to get the work done, the team members have to support each other. Employees acknowledge that they are both a customer and a supplier to others within the company. People working in teams will work together to gain a better understanding of processes and work out and resolve issues and problems when they arise. People in management will constantly look for ways of reducing the possibility of the problems and improving and offering the best possible service. This will be helped by providing effective and continual training and development for employees.

The effect of teamwork does not stop there, as the commitment of working in this way will expand to include suppliers. A company needs to acknowledge that it is reliant on suppliers, whether it supplies a direct service to its customers, such as delivery of good or services direct to the company such as toilet rolls, stationery or telephone connections. A company needs to look at suppliers as 'partner'. Working together as a team, suppliers are likely to be more motivated, extending a good quality service to the company and its customers. A company should never forget that its success is always directly connected to the happiness of its customers. This is a smart, logical way of working with suppliers and customers alike. Both suppliers and customers play an important part in the company's success.

Employees who work in companies with traditional hierarchical management can feel unable to try out new ways and new things. They may feel unable to use their own initiative and feel unable to make use of their full abilities without the fear of retribution from their superiors. Employees may also feel unable to express themselves or apply their full ability to their jobs or tasks. Poor management will quite often assert authority over employees introducing and enforcing meaningless policies that have no value or real purpose. This type of management does not make sense and is counter-productive. It creates an unnatural emphasis on status within a company, which in turn creates the need for subordinates, producing a 'them and us' situation.

To establish an open, no-blame culture, people need to believe that there is co-operation between all employees – no matter what position they hold within the company. Of course, the aim of implementing a quality culture within a company is to change attitudes and to reinforce productivity and skill of exceptional service. This helps promote a culture where people pull out all the stops to work together for everyone's benefit.

People do, of course, have different levels of responsibility than others. In a contact centre environment, team leaders will oversee and support advisers in their role in addition to monitoring their performance. It is the way in which this is handled, the approach and attitude of the team leaders to the adviser which is an important factor. Team leaders need to make advisers feel that they are an important part of the company and that working together as a team adds enormous value for all involved, not just the company but also themselves and the customers. To do so, team leaders need to use their abilities to support the interests of their team openly and consistently.

Providing good customer service can be difficult to say the least. There are five factors that are key to quality service:

- Tangibles – *Those things that are physical should send the right messages to customers. For a contact centres this could be brochures mailed in the post, the look of the website and ease of access to the systems and the advisers.*

- Reliability – *The adviser's ability to perform the services efficiently and effectively. The adviser needs to be able to communicate effectively in a business-like yet friendly and helpful manner. The chances are that the customer will recognise that the adviser has really listened, understood and appreciated their situation. The customer will be satisfied with the response and that all his concerns have been dealt with to his satisfaction.*

- Responsiveness – *The adviser's willingness to help customers and provide a prompt service. Of course it is not always possible to fulfil every customer's requirement. When this is the case advisers be need to creative in what they can say that will not disappoint the customer.*

Question

What can an adviser say to a customer that will not disappoint them?

The adviser can say, for example, 'Unfortunately, it's not possible for us to do that, but we can look at some alternative options for you' or 'that's not something this company offers, however, we do have some alternatives that you may wish to look at' or what about 'Sorry, I can't help you but I can give you the details of someone who may be able to help', or 'I don't know the answer to that, however, if you would like to hold, I'll find out for you'. By going that little bit further, gives customers confidence that the adviser has listened and tried to help.

- Assurance – *the adviser's knowledge and skill and their ability to inspire trust and confidence. The adviser needs to communicate in such as way as the customer can tell this. For example in terms of a telephone call the adviser that has a strong confident tone will inspire much more trust that one who is very quietly spoken and hesitant.*
- Empathy – *the adviser's ability to show the customer that they care about the customer as an individual. The ability to view and understand the position from other people's perspective, is an important attribute. People who have the ability to look at things from the perspective of other employees, the company as a whole and customers are a great asset. It says they have a sense of appreciation of problems others may have. It says that they will not instantly judge the abilities or behaviour of others based on their own views. Without this ability people will struggle to communicate effectively or co-operate and work easily with others, whether colleagues or customers.*

You will see that these are mostly about the 'people' element of the marketing mix. Back up for these people is highly important. They require good products, training, IT, premises, processes and systems to be able to deliver an effective service.

The tensions arise when the organisation varies other parts of the marketing mix so potentially making delivery of the service more difficult for advisers.

Question

How can the marketing mix be varied which could cause problems in delivering service by the contact centre adviser?

Examples could be:

- *difference in pricing – cost increases often lead to customer complaints which advisers need to be able to handle;*
- *cost cuts leading to reduced service, a smaller number of advisers dealing with the same number of enquiries; and*
- *product changes leading to increased numbers of enquiries for advisers to deal with as well as understanding the product changes themselves.*

In today's world of business, organisational structures are based around teams, processes and projects. Today, technology replaces the need for people to help co-ordinate and dispense information to those only who need it. Technology allows employees to directly access all the information and make contact with the people they need to in order to do their work effectively and efficiently. There is no longer the need for middle managers to dispense information to employees when they can locate the information they need at the touch of a button.

In the contact centre environment, it has become vital for companies to allow agents access to information on the company's sales, customer needs, orders and how well people and teams are doing. Letting agents know how well their team is doing encourages teamwork and promotes competitiveness for them to do well.

Employees have access to more information than ever before. Information and knowledge is key to the work that most people do. Employees will use the information to help them understand the current position of the company and will use this as a guide for direction of where and what they will do next. This does not mean that companies need to issue reports every week or month. It does not mean that companies needs to give every employee information on everything about the company. Companies should make employees aware of what information is available and that it is up to the employee to take advantage of this and to be aware of how they are contributing to quality service.

Unit 4

The Basic Rights of Contact Centre Customers

4.1
Describe the elements of law on which customers rights are founded

There are many different definitions of what the words 'the law' means. Some of these definitions are easier to understand than others.

> **Question**
>
> What do you think the words 'the law' mean?

Essentially, law is a set of rules instituted by acts of Parliament, custom or practice applying to individuals and corporate bodies in order to deal with those people who break the conventions of society. English law can be divided into *criminal* law and *civil* law. The basic differences between them are as follows.

Criminal law:

- *Breaking the rules may result in the prosecution of the offender.*
- *These rules deal with behaviour which the state disapproves of.*
- *Cases are heard in criminal courts; magistrates' court or the crown court.*
- *Punishment may involve fines or imprisonment.*
- *The parties involved will be either the Crown or the Police versus the defendant.*

Civil law:

- *Breaking the rules may result in the defender being sued.*
- *These rules relate to disputes between individuals or corporate bodies.*
- *Cases are heard in civil courts; the county court or high court.*
- *The parties involved are the **plaintiff** and **defendant**.*
- *The defendant may have to pay compensation/damages to the plaintiff.*

Law may be divided in four main types:

- common law – *this is a judge-made system of law originally based on local custom and now applied uniformly throughout England;*
- equity – *equity literally means fairness or justice, therefore the essential point of equity is to establish what is fair in a particular case at the expense of technical niceties. This can sometimes be in conflict with common law however equity law will prevail;*
- statute – *This is where an Act of Parliament creates a new rule of conduct. It passed by Parliament and can only be repealed by Parliament; and*
- EC law – *this is created by either regulations which are binding on all EC member states without Parliamentary legislation or by Directives which require member states to pass national laws within a certain time period.*

4.1.1 *Contract law*

This next section deals with the law of contract.

Question

How would you define a contract?

A contract can be described as an agreement between two or more parties, especially one that is written and enforceable by law to deliver goods or services or to do something on mutually agreed terms. Generally a contract may be written, oral or even 'implied' by conduct or action. This may be surprising as most people think a contract is a large and difficult document to read and understand. However, some types of contract must be in writing and in a particular format, e.g. for the sale of land.

For a contract to be valid it must contain the following elements:

- offer and acceptance – *this means that there must be evidence that the first party made an offer of goods or services to the second party and that the second party accepted the conditions;*
- an intention to create a legal relationship – *this is a complex area however put simply, domestic agreements cannot be enforced unless there is proof of an intention to create legal relations. In commercial agreements it is presumed that that parties intend to make an agreement unless there is evidence that legal relations were not intended;*
- consideration – *this is defined as any form of remuneration or encouragement of value given by one person to the other to persuade them to enter into the contract. More often than not this is in the form of money;*
- capacity to contract – *a person's ability to enter into a legal contract may be affected by their contractual capacity. The main groups here are:*
  - *minors (those people under the age of 18);*
  - *registered companies – these are legal entities in their own right governed by their 'memorandum of association' which sets out what powers to contract the company has;*
  - *persons who are insane or drunk;*
- Reality of consent – *to be valid a contract must also have real consent by all parties to the contract. The contract may be rendered invalid by any misrepresentation, mistake, duress (pressure or coercion), undue influence or fraud. Another point is that as a general rule persons who are not party to the contract cannot sue any of the parties to the contract concerning matters contained within it;*
- legality of object – *it is not possible to make contracts which are illegal, for an immoral purpose or which are contrary to public policy (broadly, against the public interest). There cannot be a contract to commit a criminal act for example.*

The final area to consider in relation to contact law is how the contract may be terminated. A contract ends or is 'discharged' when the 'obligations' (duties or requirements) contained within it cease to be binding. This may occur in one of four ways:

- by agreement – *if there is a subsequently a new contract or if there are clauses within it which trigger automatic discharge relating to a certain point in time or the occurrence of a particular event such;*
- by performance – *if all the parties have met all their promises or obligations in full, on time and correctly then the contract will be discharged by performance such as the provision of a holiday by a travel company;*
- By frustration – *if it is impossible for the obligations to be met beyond the control of the parties then the contract is frustrated and therefore discharges. This could be due to freak weather conditions delaying air travel; or*
- by breach – *in this instance the promises made in the contract have been broken and the innocent party to the contract can treat the contract as discharged.*

Here is a simple example. Mr Smith agrees with Mr Jones to buy his lawnmower for £50 and they shake hands on it. Mr Jones believes therefore that Mr Smith will pay £50 on delivery of the lawnmower.

Question

Has there been offer and acceptance here?

There has been offer and acceptance.

Question

What is the consideration to be?

The consideration is £50.

Question

When will the contract be discharged?

When Mr Jones delivers the lawnmower and Mr Smith hands over £50.

In the commercial world where a consumer contracts with a large and powerful organisation, the concept that a contract is reliant on an agreement, can happen where one party is in a better or stronger position than the other. The effect is that the organisation can impose terms on the consumer. For example, the majority of companies will have a standard contract with terms and conditions of sale of its products and services. Customers will be bound under the terms and conditions of this contract, whether they are aware of them or not. It can be the case that customers are completely unaware that they have entered an agreement or have do so unwillingly. This is why it is very important that customers' attention is brought to terms and conditions so that they can understand the nature of the agreement they are entering into. A person becomes a customer of a financial services provider as soon as an account is opened. Often the account opening form is the written contract that sets out the 'banker-customer' relationship.

4.1.2 Agency law

An *agency* is in effect a contract whereby one person, the 'principal', contracts with another person, the 'agent', with the objective that the agent will act on behalf of the principal to undertake certain activities.

Question

What are common examples of agency?

Common examples of agency are those such as where an estate agent is hired to sell people's houses, where an auctioneer sells goods on behalf of vendors or where a financial services provider will act as an agent for an insurance company selling their insurance products.

In the estate agent example there are three parties and two contracts. Consider person (A) is selling their house to purchaser (B) using estate agent (C). The two contractual relationships exist between:

- *A as vendor (seller) to B, the purchaser; and*
- *A as principal to C, the agent.*

To be a valid agency relationship the principal must have full contractual capacity. However this is not necessarily the case with the agent.

An agency may be created verbally or by written agreement and may relate to one or a series of transactions. Essentially there are six ways of creating an agency, discussed below.

- By consent – *this may either be express or implied authority. An express authority is where the principal instructs the agents either verbally or in writing, as in the estate agent example. An implied authority is where it is assumed that the agent has authority. Where such implied authority is usual then in law the principal will be liable for the agent's actions.*
- By statute – *this is where laws affect the formation of agency such as the Partnership Act 1890 where the partners act as agents for each other.*
- By apparent authority – *this is where an agent exceeds his 'actual' authority. These actions however are of a type that an agent would normally have the authority to undertake. The principal is bound by the limits of either the actual or apparent authority whichever is the wider.*
- Of necessity – *this could be where there is an emergency and a decision has to be made. This type of agency can be established provided the four following conditions are met:*
  - *the agent has control of the property in question;*
  - *there was a real emergency;*
  - *the principal could not be contacted;*
  - *the agent acted honestly in the best interests of the principal.*
  Imagine the example of where Mrs Brown owns a coffee shop. She goes on holiday and employs a manager to run the shop whilst she is away. Unfortunately a water pipe bursts in the shop and the manager cannot contact Mrs Brown. The manager can, out of necessity to the on-going business of the coffee shop, authorise a plumber to carryout repairs and incur costs on Mrs Brown's behalf.
- By ratification – *If person has acted without authority but these actions are subsequently ratified or confirmed by the principal then the principal becomes bound by any transactions which have occurred.*

The main duties of a principal are to:

- *pay the agent for undertaking duties; and*
- *pay all related expenses and to indemnify (cover) the agent against loss, costs, liabilities in undertaking his/her duties.*

In the contractual relationship between the principal and the agent the duties of one are the rights of the other.

An agent has five main responsibilities to their principal, namely to:

- *obey any instructions given by the principal;*
- *perform their duties personally, i.e. he cannot delegate his authority except in certain circumstances;*
- *use reasonable care and skill;*
- *act in good faith; and*
- *keep proper accounts for inspection by the principal.*

The ways of terminating an agency are similar to those in contact law discussed in the last section.

Banks act as agents for their customers when they pay (debit from the customer's account) or collect (process a cheque paid into the customer's account) a cheque. The bank owes the customer a duty of care and may be liable if it pays away funds on a customer's cheque that has been fraudulently altered.

4.1.3 What remedies are available to customers or organisations under contract law?

The Unfair Contract Terms Act 1977 and the Unfair Contract Terms Directive deal with the terms of certain contracts for the sale of goods and are examples of where legislation can severely restrict the ability of providers and substantially protect the individual. Contracts of insurance however, are exempt from the 1977 Act. The Act curtails the use of terms which try to exclude liability on the part of the provider and which try to restrict the rights of the individual. The Directive applies to life and pensions contracts. Any unfair term – one that causes the significant imbalance in the parties' rights and obligations to the detriment of the consumer – is not binding on the consumer, but the rest of the contract can continue to bind both parties.

The Supply of Goods and Services Act 1982 applies to all contracts involving the supply of services. It implies three terms into such contracts, which are:

- *that the service will be performed with reasonable care and skill;*
- *if no time limit is set in the contract, work will be done in a reasonable time; and*
- *if no price is fixed a reasonable charge will be made.*

However if things do go wrong there are two types of remedies available for breach of contract, 'judicial' and 'non-judicial' remedies. Judicial remedies are those where the parties are required to go before a court of law or an arbitrator. Judicial remedies can also be divided again into criminal and civil remedies. Sometimes the same conduct may amount to a breach of contract as well as a criminal offence.

A breach of contract does not normally involve any criminal liability, simply a civil wrong and will be concerned with civil remedies for breach. Under civil remedies, the injured party can claim for specific relief, damages or restitution. For example, a customer (the injured party) may claim compensation because he believes that he has not received the agreed service from a company he employed to build his conservatory. Such compensation would take the form of damages in money.

A claim for 'restitution' can be applied when, for example, a customer has made a payment in advance but does not receive any goods from the supplier and may claim the return of his money. Whenever a contract is broken, damages are always available and can be claimed as a right. Claims for damages differ from claims for specific relief or restitution as these are left to the discretion of the court and other restrictions may be applied. The injured party does not have to prove any loss to be entitled to nominal damage claims.

There are several principles that govern claims for substantial damages, these being: the compensatory principle; kinds of loss recoverable; valuing the loss; methods of limiting damages, penalties and liquidated damages; and advanced payments.

The *compensatory principle* is concerned with the purpose of damages to compensate the plaintiff. This principle has several important issues.

- Loss to the plaintiff – *damages are generally based on loss to the plaintiff and not on gain to the defendant. There are occasions however when the defendant will gain.*
- Meaning of loss – *in order to get substantial damages the plaintiff must be able to demonstrate that he has suffered some kind of loss. Loss in this sense would be either harm/injury to the person or the person's property, or where the plaintiff's wealth has suffered because of the breach.*
- No punitive damages – *the reason for damages for breach of contract would be to pay compensation to the plaintiff and not to punish the defendant.*
- Injury to feelings – *damages are awarded to compensate a plaintiff who has suffered an actual injury, such damages are not normally available for breach of contract.*

The *kinds of loss recoverable* principle covers different types of loss.

- Expectations – *this is the most important principle and relates to the law that protects the expectations created by a contract. Under this principle damages would be award to the plaintiff if he suffered because the other party did not 'deliver' his part of the bargain.*
- Reliance – *under this principle the plaintiff may recover costs incurred for expenses or other losses in reliance on the contract. Say for instance, a customer*

orders a wardrobe from a company, which is to be collected by the customer. The company calls the customer, advises that the item is available and makes the necessary arrangement for collection. When the customer arrives the item is not available. The customer has made an unnecessary journey and has incurred an extra expense. The customer has to make another journey to collect the item. Under the reliance principle the customer may, subject to restriction, be entitled to compensation for such 'reliance' loss.

- Restitution – *claims under this principle have been discussed previously; basically claims for restitution are concerned with a payment has been made in advance.*

The relationship between expectation, reliance and restitution claims is a somewhat complicated, however, there are three clear principles. It is often up to the plaintiff to choose which to base his claim – expectation, reliance or restitution. However, the plaintiff will not always be able to claim for loss of expectation, as it may just be speculative and therefore hard to prove. In other cases, the plaintiff may not have to make a choice between the three types of loss.

When awarding damages, the plaintiff's loss has to be looked at in terms of loss of money. This principle, *valuing the loss*, looks at the process of valuation and assessment. The relevance of market values principle looks at the damages based on difference in costs of substitute or replacement value and whether they will be based on the actual cost or difference of market value.

Some other points when considering damages to be awarded are discussed below.

- Speculative damages *may be claimed when a plaintiff believes that he has been deprived of gaining some benefit. So, where a plaintiff believes he has lost the chance of earning more money, for instance, he could bring a claim for speculative damages against the other party. Of course, in this case, the court will have to look at the expected value of the benefit and the likelihood of it actually happening.*
- Methods of limiting damages – *the plaintiff may suffer loss, which is caused by a series of events that are initially caused by a breach of contract; but this does not necessarily mean that a court of law will find the other party liable for all the loss. The court will look at whether the plaintiff could have lessened the loss suffered.*
- Remoteness – *under this principle, the loss must have arisen naturally, in the usual course of things due to a breach of contract.*
- Causation – *damages can only be claimed if there is some causal connection between the breach and the plaintiff's loss.*
- Mitigation – *plaintiffs of breach of contract claims are under a duty to mitigate their loss. In other words, the plaintiff is required to ensure that the loss he suffers is limited. The plaintiff would not be awarded damages for loss that he could or should have avoided.*

- Default of the victim – *this principle refers to plaintiffs that do not mitigate their loss, as the loss would be partly due to the fact that he failed to avoid the consequences because of the other party's breach.*

- Non-payment of money – *remedy for non-payment of a fixed sum of money when due, can be remedied by a legal action for that sum. Interest can also be recovered when a contract has a provision to do so. A court also has the power to award interest if action is taken prior to payment being made. Interest cannot be awarded by a court where payment is simply made last and there is no provision within the contract.*

- Penalties and liquidated damages – *it is very difficult to forecast the amount of damages that will be awarded for breach of contract. Often the parties will try to come to some arrangement by fixing a sum to be paid. In some cases, the estimated costs will not be a genuine prediction of the actual loss, but will purely be a way of pressurise the other party to carry out his part of the contract. This is called a penalty clause. When the parties involved fix a sum to be paid that is reasonable estimate of actual loss, this is known as liquidated damages clause.*

4.2
State the duties and rights of customers, organisations and their employees

4.2.1 *Duties and rights of the customer*

In relation to contact centres there has been little case law that has been fully tested which explores fully the duties and rights of customers. While contact centres provide a good service to customers, it is on the basis that the customer has been given numbers and security codes by which he can be identified and the computer system can process the customer's requests. It must be understood that any breaches of confidentiality or misuse of the system is the customer's responsibility as much as the provider.

The main Acts which are thought to be relevant are:

- *The Supply of Goods and Services Act 1982 which deals with the care and standard of service provided (see section 4.1.3).*

- *The Bills of Exchange Act 1882, for financial service providers this Act is very important as it relates to cheques and payments of funds to and from customers' accounts.*

There is also the issue of negligence and in the legal sense this is different to the common usage of the word, i.e. something has gone wrong unintentionally. There are three essential matters that a plaintiff must prove if he is going to be successful in proving that a defendant was negligent, that:

- *a duty of care existed;*
- *there has been a breach of that duty; and*
- *some loss or damage has been sustained as a result.*

There is the case of 'contributory' negligence where a plaintiff claims for compensation, however, this claim is reduced because both parties have been considered to be negligent. Such an example may be where a customer inadvertently allows a third party access to his security codes and this third party uses this information to obtain details from the contact centre.

However, before seeking costly legal redress the customers of financial service providers have the right to complain about the services supplied by their bank. There are several steps that a customer must take. Customers first need to complain directly to their financial services provider. The customer should always make a note of the person they speak to and record details of the conversation that took place. If, after discussion, the customer is not happy with the way in which the complaint was handled or if they are not happy with the information received, they have the right to contact the most senior person within the company.

It is normal for customers to put their complaint in writing, this will set out their stall and will give their provider the opportunity of putting the problems right. Customers should always keep details of their contact with the bank. The customer should retain copies of all relevant documents for referral at a later date if necessary.

If the customer is still not satisfied and their provider cannot offer a solution after a period of six months a position of 'deadlock' is said to be reached. In this instance the customer may refer the complaint to the Financial Ombudsman Service (FOS).

Question

Who is the Financial Service Ombudsman (FOS)?

How can the FOS help customers who have a complaint?

The Financial Ombudsman Service (FOS) deals with complaints about most financial products and services provided in the UK. This includes insurance, pensions, bank accounts, investments mortgages and so on. The FOS helps when a consumer believes that a financial services company has acted wrongly and may be involved in adjudicating in the dispute. The FOS can therefore help when a consumer believes that he has lost out financially as a result. The FOS is only able to make decisions that bind an organisation to compensate the customer. Any compensation given will relate to actual loss they have incurred. There is a maximum compensation limit of £100,000.

If needs be, the complaint can then be resolved through the courts, or by 'arbitration' which is a cheaper alternative to legal proceedings. However, customers are advised that if an Ombudsman has not found in their favour then it is unlikely that a judge would overturn that judgment.

However, the FOS will not deal with any complaint case unless the consumer has already tried to resolve the issue with the company itself. The consumer must have evidence that they have reported the problem to the company, giving them the opportunity to correct the problem. The company should send a letter known as a 'final response' to the customer explaining the outcome of their investigation and the right to complain to the FOS if they are still not happy. Then, and only then, will the FOS step in. In general complaint should be made to the FOS within six months of the date of the 'final response' letter. The service is provided free of charge to consumers with complaints.

Complaints made to the FOS are not normally dealt with in a court of law. Decisions are normally reached on based on the paperwork and information supplied by the consumer and the company. In the main most complaints are resolved without the need for face-to-face meetings.

4.2.2 Have a knowledge of the duties and rights of the organisation and their employees

In the financial services sector the duties and rights of the organisation and their employees are governed by the Banking Code.

Question

What is the Banking Code?

The Banking Code is a voluntary code of practice drawn up by the British Bankers Association, the Building Societies Association and the Association for Payment Clearing Services in 1992 to set standards of good practice which should be followed as a minimum. It has been revised four times, most recently in 2000. It is to be observed by banks, building societies and card issuers in their dealings with personal customers. A personal customer, in this instance, is defined as a private individual who holds an account or uses services offered by that financial services provider. The account can be a joint account with another private individual, or the customer as an executor or a trustee may hold it. **Contact centre staff should obtain a copy of the Code as it is very important for those working in customer-facing roles.**

Compliance to the Code is handled by the Banking Code Standards Board (BCSB).

The Code has 11 key comments. Under the Code financial services providers will:

- *act fairly and reasonably;*
- *ensure that all services and products comply with the Code, even if they have their own terms and conditions;*
- *give information on services and products in plain language, and offer help if there is any aspect which the customer does not understand;*
- *help customers to choose a product or service to fit their needs;*
- *help customers to understand the financial implications of:*
  - *a mortgage;*
  - *other borrowing;*
  - *savings and investment products;*
  - *card products;*
- *help customers understand how their account works;*
- *have safe, secure and reliable banking and payment systems;*
- *ensure that the procedures staff follow reflect these commitments;*
- *correct errors and handle complaints speedily;*
- *consider cases of financial difficulty and mortgage arrears sympathetically and positively; and*
- *ensure that all services and products comply with relevant laws and regulations.*

Financial services providers must also comply with relevant legislation, judicial decisions and other codes of conduct applicable to their businesses.

Customers must be provided in writing with relevant information about products and services including charges and rates of interest, operation of accounts, lending criteria and the rules regarding credit facilities. This information is usually provided when the account is opened but should also be available upon request.

Confidentiality of customer information

Under the Banking Code financial services providers are required to treat all customer details in the strictest confidence and not to disclose information to a third party without the customer's consent, unless there is a overriding legal requirement to do so.

The are four situations in which disclosure is permitted:

- *if the customer requests or consents to disclosure;*
- *if the financial services provider is legally compelled to do so, examples being in connection with drug-trafficking and the prevention of terrorism;*
- *if it is in the financial service provider's interests to disclose, for instance if the customer has defaulted on loan repayments, the customers is given 28 days' notice before the default is registered with a credit reference agency; and*
- *if there is a duty to the public to disclose, for example if a customer is trading with an enemy at a time of war.*

Employees must take care not to disclose customer information inadvertently. They should not talk about customers' accounts among themselves outside work or to their friends or relatives. The also extends to taking documentation about customers off the premises and taking care to dispose of customer documentation in the correct way.

There are some other aspects of the Banking Code which are important as discussed below:

- Marketing of services – *financial service providers cannot justify disclosing customer details to a third party for marketing purposes by claiming that it is in the organisation's best interest. They must have the customer's written consent to pass the customer's name to a third party within a marketing group. Organisations are also not allowed to make the provision of a service, such as opening a bank account, conditional of giving this consent.*

  When the customer opens an account, the financial services provider must give the customer the chance to say he does not want to receive marketing literature.

  When a financial services provider advertises its lending services it must make clear that applications for loans will be subject to appraisal of the customer's financial standing. The advertising and promotional literature must be fair and reasonable with no misleading information.

- Handling customer complaints – *under the Code financial services providers must establish internal procedures for handling customer complaints in a fair and timely manner and inform customers of these procedures. Staff dealing directly with customers must also be aware of how to handle these complaints. Financial service providers must belong to one of the authorised Ombudsman or arbitration schemes such as the Banking Ombudsman/Building Societies Ombudsman, which is now overseen by the Financial Services Authority.*

Financial service providers have a duty to inform customers of the interest rates that apply to their accounts and when interest will be paid or deducted. When interest rates are changed, how the information will be conveyed is important. Under the Banking Code, changes in interest rates should be conveyed on telephone helplines, websites and in branches within three working days. Providers are also required to inform customers of any day-to-day charges for running their accounts or services, including charges made for using cash machines.

All terms and conditions have to be fair and set out the customers rights and their responsibilities in a clear and easy to read manner. Use of technical or legal jargon should only be used where necessary. Financial institutions need to ensure that customers read the terms and conditions so that they understand the commitment that is being made. Equally, financial service providers need to advise customers of how they will be informed of any changes to the terms and conditions. Changes that are in the customer's advantage must be conveyed to them within 30 days, although the provider may make the change immediately. Changes that disadvantage the customer must be conveyed to the customer personally at least 30 days prior to the bank making the change.

Customers who are not happy with a current or savings account should be allowed a cooling off period whereby the bank will make arrangements to refund all the money, including any interest gained or help the customer to move to another account. Under the Banking Code, this cooling-off period is 14 days from the customer making their first payment into the account.

4.3
Explain the need to protect customers, organisations and their employees

There are a number of areas in which protection of customers, organisations and their employees is required. These are for instance in the areas of:

- *financial loss;*
- *information – its use and security;*
- *payments – for goods and services and the repayment of debts; and*
- *fraud – its prevention, detection and reduction.*

Question

Why is there a need for protection?

Customers need to be protected primarily against financial loss, as it is important that they are not put into a position of hardship. They should not unknowingly purchase a product or service that exposes them to an unacceptable level of risk had they been aware of the full facts. This might be in respect of loans they cannot afford to repay or investments that are too speculative. The Consumer Credit Act 1974 and the Financial Services and Markets Act 2000 respectively cover these two examples.

Organisations should be responsible and conduct their business in an ethical and socially responsible manner. Therefore they require policy guidelines to inform processes and procedures to ensure the ongoing business success.

Employees need to take care that they do not give information which may be considered misleading, and encourage the customer to take goods or services that are not suitable for their needs. There are other regulations, for example relating to money laundering, in which employees can become personally liable. This means that employees need to follow internal procedures that have been designed for their protection.

In relation to the examples given above, financial service providers need to ensure that they treat all personal information held on customers, past and present, as confidential. No details including name, address or information on customer accounts should be disclosed other than that as required by law, or it the company believes that it is in their own interest to do so, or that there is a duty to the public to do so. The Data Protection Act 1998 (considered in Section 4.5) deals with how information should be used and stored.

If an individual is unable to make payment and the amount owed is not in dispute or following formal demand for repayment is still not made, companies may disclose information on the debts to credit reference agencies in order to protect other companies. However, in order to help and protect the individual, the company must give at least 28 days' notice of their intention to inform the credit reference agencies. The company should advise the individual of the role of the credit reference agencies and what the effect on them will be personally, i.e. that informing the credit reference agency of outstanding debts may result in the individual's ability to gain further credit in the future.

Customers also have a duty to protect themselves against fraud by ensuring that they take care of cheque books, cards, electronic purse, PINs and other security information. Customers need to ensure that they inform their provider immediately they are aware of any cards or cheque books, etc, that have been lost or stolen in order to reduce the loss. When credit or debit cards have been lost or stolen customers need to work with the company investigate the matter and this may involve the police. Customers will generally be limited to a liability payment of £50.00 regardless of the amount transactions made on stolen credit or debit, unless the company can prove that the customer has acted without reasonable care or acted fraudulently.

4.4
State the types of customer and the differences between them

There are four main types of customer.

Question

What are these different types of customer?

The different types of customers are personal, business, clubs and charities, and minors. They are divided into different customer groups because of the legal frame-works that surround them. It is also useful for financial service providers to use this as a basis for initial segmentation of the customer market.

4.4.1 *Personal customers*

Personal customers are private individuals who can open either sole accounts – where a customer holds the account in their own name only – or joint accounts – where two, or more, customers hold an account together. In this instance the customers sign a 'mandate' which sets out the signing instructions and liability on the account should it become overdrawn. Personal customers are normally offered such services as cheque accounts, online banking and overdraft facilities.

As we have seen, several different statutes protect personal customers. The Data Protection Act 1998 determines how personal data is handled and stored. The Supply of Goods and Service Act 1982 states that goods and service have to correspond with the description given, be of satisfactory quality and be fit for purpose. The Banking Code is there to help ensure that banks and building societies perform to set standards. Additionally, the Financial Ombudsman Service is available free of charge to personal customers of financial services company that have a complaint.

4.4.2 *Business*

Banking for businesses is a necessity. There are three main types of business:

* sole trader – *a business account where the customer owns their own business;*
* partnership – *a group of people running a business together, e.g. a doctors' practice, firms of accountants or solicitors. The partnership is not a separate legal entity but a number of people conducting business together under a trading name;* and
* Limited company – *this again is a group of persons running a business, however the limited company has a legal entity in its own right – this is known as being 'incorporated', i.e. that they have a certificate to prove that the company exists and is registered as such.*

The signing instructions and other activities relating to the account are covered by a mandate. It is important that these mandates are kept up-to-date as personnel join and leave organisations and the financial service provider could inadvertently be paying cheques signed by someone who was not recorded on their mandate.

Most financial service providers will segment business by 'turnover' that is the amount of income they generate in a financial year. This gives segment names of 'small business', 'corporate' and 'large corporate'. These businesses benefit from many services apart from the normal current account, such as an account or relationship manager, corporate/business credit cards, overdraft facilities and different types of accounts. Contract law, amongst others, covers business banking.

4.4.3 Clubs and charities

The Charities Act 1993 controls clubs and charities. This Act defines the way in which the organisation operates. The club or charity set their own rules when the organisation is initiated which they then need to follow in the normal course of operation. The services offered are similar to that of a business account. All bank accounts, cheque books and so forth have to be in the club or charity's name. Signatories will be nominated and only those people will be able to sign cheques or deal with the bank. The way in which the account or other services is run will be governed by the rules of the club or charity.

4.4.4 Minors

A minor is defined as a person under the age of 18. These customers generally are unable to enter into contracts, other than to pay for necessities, or contracts that are to their benefit, such as contracts of employment. This means that if financial services providers were to lend to a minor, they would not be able to recover any moneys should the customer be unable to repay them. This means that usually minors are not able to arrange overdrafts or loans. An exception might be if they could arrange a parent or guardian to 'guarantee' the loan for them.

4.5
Explain the data protection legislation and what this means for organisations and employees

The Data Protection Act 1998 basically regulates the use of personal information held on computers and within manual records. The previous Act of 1984 only offered protection to information held on the computer. The Act works in two ways, it:

- *gives individuals certain rights; and*
- *gives those that record and use the information – known as data controllers under the Act – certain guidelines to follow. These practices are known as the 'Data Protection Principles'.*

Question

What does personal information mean?

Personal information is data about living and identifiable individuals. The information does not necessarily have to be sensitive and can be as little as a name and address.

The three key principles of the Act are:

- *a customer has the right to know if an individual or company has information relating to them;*
- *the customer has the right to see that information and the company or individual holding such information has to reply to such requests within 40 days. The request may be verbal or written; and*
- *that the customer has the right to have the information erased or corrected if appropriate. Compensation is available to individuals who suffer damage by incorrect use of their data, its inaccuracy or unauthorised disclosure.*

When the Act makes reference to data controllers it refers to those that control the manner and purpose in which the personal data is process. Data controllers could therefore be any type of company within the public or private sector, a partnership or a sole trader or indeed an individual. In order to demonstrate compliance with the Act each data controller must have a 'Data Protection Policy'.

The Information Commissioner is responsible for administering and enforcing the Data Protection Act 1998. The Information Commissioner is an independent official appointed by the Queen and who reports directly to Parliament. The Information Commissioner's office deals with the matters relating to the Data Protection Act for the whole of the UK.

Any organisation or individual that processes personal information is required to notify the Information Commissioner of that fact. The size of the organisation is immaterial, what is important is the personal information that is held in relation to the business activities. Organisations that fail to notify the Information Commissioner may find themselves facing heavy fines in the Magistrates Court or higher.

By following the Data Protection Principles of the Act companies will set themselves a good set of operating practices through good information handling. The Data Protection Act has eight Data Protection principles that need to be followed by companies. These are that data is:

- obtained fairly and lawfully;
- held only for specific and lawful purposes;
- Relevant, adequate and only for the purpose for which it is required – *the quantity of the data needs to be checked and monitored regularly to ensure this is being held for the purpose of the business and they do not hold too much or too little data about the individuals. For instance, a financial service provider*

may frequently collect date of birth information on its existing customers. When they reach 18 the company will target them with marketing material for a credit card or a personal loan. Whereas other companies will only need to know that individuals are over the age of 18;

- accurate and where necessary kept up-to-date – *data controllers should only collect and retain information that is actually required and that it is accurate. Data controllers need to ensure that inaccurate data is corrected as quickly as possible;*

- not kept any longer than necessary – *data controllers should also ensure that collected information is not held indefinitely. Data should be continually monitored and after a certain period removed from the system. For example, when Mrs Jacks completed the payment of her personal loan and is no longer a customer of the finance company, her details should be removed from the system that would automatically send marketing information to her;*

- processed in accordance with the individual's rights – *data controllers that use personal information for direct marketing need to ensure that the individuals are aware of the fact. Data controllers have to allow individuals the chance to opt out of having their information used in this way. The Information Commissioner receives numerous complaints about companies that have used personal data in an unfair in way. In order remain legal, data controllers should set up and maintain a list of all the individuals that choose not to receive marketing material. The list should be checked prior to any marketing campaigns being conducted by the data controllers;*

- kept secure – *security of data is a major issue for both the data controller and the individual. The onus is on the data controllers to ensure that everything within its power is done to ensure that personal information is kept secure. Data controllers need to think about the damage that could be caused to the individual if their personal information was disclosed or lost through inadequate security.*

Data controllers need to ensure that only those employees that are permitted gain access to personal information of individuals; this can be achieved through a series of passwords that are issued to authorised personnel. To insure against misuse, passwords should be changed on a regular basis. Procedure documentation should be set up which lists which employees are authorised to access information, why and for what purpose. Disciplinary procedures should be put in place for any employee that is found to misuse personal information.

Question

How often are you required to change your password?

The prevention of accidental loss or theft of personal data must be treated a serious concern by any data controller. Although companies can put in place procedures and passwords to deal with the general day to day issues of safekeeping of data, what about the unexpected, unanticipated events such as fire or theft? Companies need to ensure that back-up copies of files is kept in secure preferably in an area, which they are not normally used and that the actual computer system and equipment is physically secured; and

- transferred only to countries outside the UK that offer adequate protection – *data controllers are permitted to transfer data to countries outside of the EEA (the European Union and Norway, Iceland and Liechtenstein). However, they will need to ensure that the data receives adequate protection in that country or that the individual has agreed the release of the information to that country.*

Basically, the principles of the Data Protection Act require that data controllers process information in a fair way. That means that when information is collected from individuals the data controller is open and honest about what it will be used for and they must have a legitimate reason for processing it. Additionally, they will need to explain who they are, what they intend to do with the information and who they intend to give the information to.

Complying with the Data Protection Principles will help companies to limit or eradicate complaints from the general public on how they process the information they hold on individuals. It is therefore in the interest of the company that they understand individual's rights and comply.

Companies need to ensure that employees are aware of individual's rights. More importantly, employees need to the ability to recognise when an access request is being made and how important it is that they deal with and act upon the request urgently.

4.6
Describe the telephone preference service and the impact on contact centre operations

Most companies within the financial services industry will regularly conduct some type of telesales or telemarketing campaigns. Some believe this to be the most effective way of keeping existing customers up-to-date with new products and services and of introducing themselves to new and potential customers.

However, since 1995 it has been illegal for companies to make direct contact with customers whether existing or potential that have registered a desire not to receive unsolicited calls. In 1995 the Direct Marketing Association (DMA) set up the Telephone Preference Service (TPS). The Telephone Preference Service was originally formed, as a voluntary, self-regulatory scheme to control unsolicited telephone calls. The basic idea was to make it possible for the general public to register their desire not to receive unwanted telephone calls from companies wishing to promote and sell their products and services.

In 1997, following the implementation of the Telecommunications Data Protection Directive by the European Parliament, the Department of Trade and Industry and the Office of Telecommunications (OFTEL) entered into public consultation. As a result, 1999 saw the emergence of the Telecommunication (Data Protection and Privacy) Regulations. These new Regulations came into effect on 1 May 1999.

Earlier in 1999, OFTEL invited companies to bid for the management of the scheme, which at that time was more commonly known as the Telephone Opt-Out scheme. The contract was award to the DMA, who now run and manage the scheme under the banner of the Telephone Preference Service (TPS).

By registering their details with the TPS, individuals can eliminate unwanted and unsolicited calls. Companies that carry out any type of telesales or telemarketing activity have the ability to receive these details by subscribing to the TPS. Additionally, when an individual tells a company that their calls are not welcomed and they did not wish to receive further calls from them, the company must ensure that this wish is adhered to and remove or added the details their 'do not call' list. Companies must adhere to the individual's request within 28 days of notification. Therefore all companies that make telesales or telemarketing calls are required to ensure that they 'clean' their list to ensure that they comply with the regulations. This means that they have to ensure that no individual is contacted that has registered 28 days or more previously with the TPS or with the company directly. It is important that employees only use those names that have been cleared against the list. This may be the responsibility of the employee or the marketing department of the organisation.

An individual has the right to complain about any company that contacts them, if they have registered their objection. This can be done either direct to the Office of the Data Protection Commissioner who is responsible for the enforcement of the Regulations, or with the TPS. Complaints received by the TPS who will investigate and file a full report to the Office of the Data Protection Commissioner.

Index

function, role of, 61
goals and objectives, 69
key elements, 62
management process of, 61
market-coverage strategies, 73, 74
matching process, as, 62
mix, 65
    variation of, 93, 94
needs and wants of customers, meeting,
    70
objectives, 64
people, importance of, 65, 66
product, 65
products and services, of, 68–71
promotion, 65
right price, deciding on, 65
sales campaigns, considerations, 69
segmentation, 74–76
selling, and, 60, 62
strategies, 66, 67
strengths and opportunities, comparing,
    63
SWOT analysis, 63, 64
trends, 67, 68
Minors
customers, as, 113
Mobile phones
Global System for Mobile, 24
Small Message Service, 24, 25
Wireless Application Protocol. *See*
    WIRELESS APPLICATION
    PROTOCOL
Multimedia Message Service
use of, 26

Negligence
contributory, 105
elements of, 104

Personal finance
accessibility and flexibility, 6
communication, means of, 6
Powerdiallers
use of, 29, 30

Private Automatic Branch Exchange
    System
use of, 29
Products
comparison of, 78
marketing, 68–71
meaning, 70

Quality culture
benefits of, 87
creation of, 87
need for, 86–88
quality, measuring, 88–90
quality service, 86
resistance to, 86, 87
service quality control, 90
Queues
assessment, 56, 57
content, 56
customers and contact centres
    measurements, relationship of, 54, 55
intelligent, 56
message, quality of, 55
practical things to do with, 57, 58
quality of, 56

Restitution
claim for, 102

Selling
marketing, and, 60, 62
Services
contract for supply of, 101
financial services sector, in, 88
marketing, 68–71
marketing strategy for, 70, 71
Shareholders
value, importance of, 13, 17, 18
Shares
Initial Public Offering, 17
Small Message Service
introduction of, 24, 25
Strategic decisions
formulation of, 4